ONCE IN A LIFETIME TRIPS

ONCE IN A LIFETIME TRIPS

THE WORLD'S 50 MOST EXTRAORDINARY AND MEMORABLE TRAVEL EXPERIENCES

CHRIS SANTELLA

Clarkson Potter/Publishers
New York

ACKNOWLEDGMENTS

This book would not have been possible without the generosity of the intrepid travelers who shared tales of their adventures. To these men and women, I offer the most heartfelt thanks. I also want to acknowledge the fine efforts of my editor, Doris Cooper, and the Clarkson Potter team, including Angelin Borsics, Maggie Hinders, Marysarah Quinn, Stephanie Huntwork, and Christine Tanigawa. Their work was instrumental in bringing this book into being. Thanks should also go to Minda Novek, who spearheaded efforts to locate the perfect photography to complement each trip; and to my agent, Stephanie Kip Rostan, who always provides sage counsel. This list would hardly be complete without a profound thank-you to my mon and dad, who encouraged me to pursue my dream of being a writer . . . and most of all to my wife, Deidre, and daughters, Cassidy Rose and Annabel Blossom, who have again and again displayed tremendous patience, flexibility, and love.

PHOTOGRAPH CREDITS

page 2: © Bob Krist/CORBIS; 5: Courtesy Taj Hotels Resorts and Palaces; 9: © Peter Adams/JAI/CORBIS; 10: Courtesy Silolona; 13: Courtesy Cruise West; 16: © Barbara Banks; 18: © Bill Abbott; 21, 22: © Brian O'Keefe; 25: © Shannon Hastings; 26: © Sandy Harford; 29: Courtesy Silolona; 33: © Jack Grove; 36: © Ethan Gordon; 41, 43: Courtesy Deep Ocean Expeditions; 44: © David Ross/Wilderness Safaris; 46: © Bob Krist/CORBIS; 51: © Inmagine/Unlisted Images, Inc.; 55: © Nancy Opitz; 56: © Didi Lotze; 59: © Dana Allen/Wilderness Safaris; 62: © Peter Guttman/CORBIS; 64, 67: © Elephant Back Safaris; 69: © Jorge Salaverri; 73: © Frans Lanting/CORBIS; 77: © Christophe Boisvieux/age fotostock; 78: © Road to Mandalay; 81: Claire Leimbach/Getty Images; 84–85: Courtesy Trans Niugini Tours; 87: © Cyril Ruoso/Minden Pictures; 89: © Andre Baertschi/wildtropix.com; 91: © Howie Garber/Animals Animals; 92: © Fritz Poelking/age footstock; 96: © B. Balik; 98: © Bilderbuch/Design Pics/CORBIS; 102: © Tai Power Seeff/Getty Images; 104–5: © Timothy Allen/Getty Images; 108: © Sylvain Grandadam/age fotostock; 111: © B. Balik; 115: Courtesy Southern Lakes Heliski; 118: © Ahmed Al-Shukaili; 123: © Peter Adams/age fotostock; 126: © Tomas Utsi/Naturfoto; 128–29: © Diane Cook & Len Jenshel/CORBIS; 133: © Jimmy Chin; 136: © Catherine Karnow/CORBIS; 139: Courtesy Voyages Longitude 131°; 143, 144: Courtesy The Westin Turnberry Resort, Scotland; 147: © Rob Howard; 150: Courtesy Equitours; 153: © Peter Adams/zefa/CORBIS; 154–55: © Arctic-Images/CORBIS; 158: © www.danheller.com; 161: © Frontiers North Adventures; 164: © Daisy Gilardini; 168: © Dennis E. Powell; 171: © Russell Young/JAI/CORBIS; 175: Courtesy Rovos Rail Tours; 178: © Alison Wright/CORBIS; 182: © Peter Adams/CORBIS; 185: Courtesy Cavas Wine Lodge; 189: © Venice Simplon-Orient-Express; 190–91: © Maurice Joseph/Alamy; 195: © Jim Zuckerman/CORBIS; 198: © Alvaro Leiva/age fotostock; 200–201: © Glowimages/age fotostock; 205: © Kamran Jebreili/age fotostock; 206: © Grapheast/age fotostock; 209: Courtesy Jumeirah; 212: © Pascal Deloche/Godong/CORBIS; 214: © Ian Black; 217: Courtesy NASA; 220: © Ian Black.

Library of Congress Cataloging-in-Publication Data

Santella, Chris.
Once in a lifetime trips / Chris Santella. —1st ed.
1. Voyages and travels. I. Title.
G465.S26   2009
910.4—dc22   2008036991

ISBN 978-0-307-40692-7

Printed in China

Design by Maggie Hinders

1 3 5 7 9 10 8 6 4 2

First Edition

To Cassidy, Annabel, and Deidre,
and all the adventures we'll share together

CONTENTS

INTRODUCTION

I F YOU WERE TO ASK A DOZEN DIFFERENT PEOPLE to describe their ultimate dream vacation—their once in a lifetime trip if time and expense were no object—you'd likely elicit a dozen different responses. For some it might be an escape to an exotic tropical paradise in Indonesia or French Polynesia—far off the grid but outfitted with all the amenities you'd expect from a five-star hotel. For others it might be the chance to venture behind the scenes at some of Europe's greatest opera houses, or go face-to-face with a mountain gorilla in Rwanda.

There's little question that the world is getting smaller, at least from a travel perspective. The proliferation of travel blogs and websites and travel programs on television can make once mystical places seem almost mundane. Though the world's most secret travel treasures and experiences may seem less secret now, the allure of that trip you've always dreamed of remains a powerful elixir. And there's nothing that can replace firsthand experience.

It was this elixir, the whimsy to move beyond the everyday to imagine some extraordinary adventures, that inspired me to write *Once in a Lifetime Trips*.

In my time writing about outdoor sports travel, I've assembled my own wish list of such trips—given my proclivities, most of them involve fly-fishing, golf, or some combination of the two. But when I set out to write this book, I realized that my biases—and my dearth of worldly experience—would severely limit the palette from which I could draw. To assemble a truly compelling list of trips, I turned to fifty passionate travelers—people whose love for a corner of the world or for a particular recreational pastime have made them authorities on the place or activity that fascinates them. (In many cases, these individuals' zeal has led them to a career in the travel field.) My field of inquiry was simple; I asked each person to tell me about a travel *experience* they were passionate about, one that they considered a "once in a lifetime" trip. I emphasize experience, as each trip presents not only a place, but also a special way to come to understand that place, and in understanding that place, perhaps come to better understand ourselves.

The Winelands region near Cape Town, South Africa, is emerging as one of the world's great wine producers.

Some of my interviewees detailed destinations and trips that they'd helped research and assemble; others spoke of trips they'd always hoped to take, then actually experienced them . . . and probably never will again. Some described extravagant venues bordering on the decadent, others recounted fragile cultures and ecosystems, believing that the best way to preserve them is by sharing them so others will understand just how precious they are. Each trip is brought to life by the detailed account of someone who has experienced the journey, and by stunning photography that animates each destination.

Trips are categorized by the type of surrounding where they unfold. A cruise to Antarctica, for example, falls in the "On the Ocean" section.

After reading *Once in a Lifetime Trips,* you may find yourself moved to begin exploring the possibility of embarking on a few of these adventures yourself. To help you begin your travels, some general planning information about each trip is provided at the end of the book.

A special trip can have many dividends. It can arouse anticipation for months in advance of your departure, create long-lasting memories, and perhaps even open hearts and minds along the way. I hope you'll be inspired to embark on a once in a lifetime trip of your own.

ON THE OCEAN

MANY OF HISTORY'S MOST EPIC ADVENTURES WERE LAUNCHED IN GREAT OCEANGOING VESSELS. THIS IS EQUALLY TRUE TODAY. Traveling by ship captures a certain exploratory bravado. There's also the fact that some places in the world that beg to be experienced—Antarctica and the most isolated islands of Micronesia come to mind—can *only* be reached by boat.

While the trips here are all ship-based, they cover a broad array of interests and visit a host of habitats. Several ("Ultimate Antarctica" and "Exploring the Galápagos") are decidedly wildlife-oriented; others mix an exploration of flora and fauna with a chance to gain a better understanding of local cultures ("In Harriman's Wake" and "Melanesia: Swimming with Mantas, Dancing with Fire"). One common denominator is the intimacy and excellence of your vessel; these are not the mega cruise ships of casinos and all-night buffets but expedition-ready vessels designed to convey a limited number of guests to out-of-the-way places in comfort. They can get places that cruise ships can't go and are equipped with the Zodiac rafts—and in one case a helicopter—necessary to get to the isolated places you'll want to explore.

The crew members of the Silolona, *a one-of-a-kind* phinisi *craft, trim the sails in the waters near the Spice Islands.*

1

In Harriman's Wake:
Circumnavigating Alaska

WHY: See nearly the entire coast of Alaska, plus the Bering Sea,
going places the big cruise ships simply can't go.

G IVEN ITS DEARTH OF ROADS AND VAST TRACTS of wilderness, it's nearly impossible to see much of Alaska by land. Not surprisingly, most tourists take in the wonders of the forty-ninth state by sea. In a busy year, nearly a million people experience Alaska's famed Inside Passage, in the southeastern section of the state, by cruise ship. It's a significantly more exclusive group—roughly 240 people a year—who have the opportunity to see the passage plus the Aleutian Islands, the Pribilofs, and the Bering Strait—what many consider to be the *real* Alaska—aboard the *Spirit of Oceanus,* on an expedition called In Harriman's Wake.

In Harriman's Wake takes adventurers on a 25-day, 3,500-mile odyssey, beginning in Vancouver, British Columbia, and concluding in Nome, Alaska, in the far north. This is not the floating shopping-mall/casino experience some might equate with cruising; guests on the *Spirit of Oceanus* are encouraged to take to the deck or descend into Zodiacs to enjoy the thundering glaciers, abundant wildlife, and majestic vistas that make coastal Alaska so awe-inspiring. "The itinerary retraces the 1899 expedition along the coast of Alaska financed by railroad magnate E. H. Harriman," says Dick West, who has worked in the Alaska travel industry most of his life. "What started out as a vacation became the largest research undertaking ever staged, with leading artists and naturalists of the day gathered to accompany Harriman and chronicle a coastal Alaska that few Americans had explored."

At 295 feet in length and accommodating a maximum of 120 passengers, the *Spirit of Oceanus* can go places that the larger cruise ships can't; it doesn't require the deep-water draft that cruise ships need, it can negotiate narrow passages, and it can change direction much more quickly. This increased flexibility allows the *Spirit* to navigate into fjords and close to islands to afford guests a more intimate Alaska experience—instead of seeing a humpback whale as a dot on the horizon, you'll be

Chukchi children on the island of Yanrakynnot in the Bering Sea.

able to make out barnacles on its fin. And you needn't compromise comfort for versatility. Each suite on the *Spirit* includes windows to take in the views, an en suite marble bathroom (with shower), and a sitting area. There are several lounges on board, a gym, and small library. Meals emphasize fresh foods, many of which are purchased from local fishermen that the *Spirit of Oceanus* encounters on the water. These include wild king and coho salmon, halibut, king crab, and mussels.

After departing Vancouver and cruising along the northern coast of British Columbia, the *Spirit of Oceanus* reaches Misty Fjords National Monument and the attractions of the Inside Passage begin to unfold. Over the next week, guests are treated to a series of glacier-fed fjords, mist-enshrouded Sitka spruce forests, and rushing waterfalls as the ship winds among the one thousand islands that buffer the mainland from the Pacific. Here the dramatic counterpoint of the sea and cliffs

You'll cruise close enough to the glaciers to hear the moan of ice stretching and cracking.

of basalt and ice that make the Alaska Panhandle so beguiling are on full display. Highlights include Frederick Sound, summer home to several hundred humpback whales that migrate from Hawaii, and Glacier Bay National Park, where on a clear day the peaks of the Fairweather Range soar high above the glaciers, which calve with a sound like a gunshot.

The *Spirit of Oceanus* next crosses the Gulf of Alaska to take in Kenai Fjords National Park. You'll cruise close enough to the glaciers to hear the moan of ice stretching and cracking. A plethora of marine mammals—Steller sea lions; sea otters; Dall porpoises; gray, humpback, minke, and killer whales (orcas)—and countless seabirds, including horned and tufted puffins, are likely to present themselves. You'll take to the Zodiacs to get a closer look. Bald eagles are a dime a dozen in this part of the world; after you've been in Alaska a few days, you'll barely bother to look up as one of these majestic birds flies overhead.

As *Spirit of Oceanus* leaves Resurrection Bay, it's all new territory as far as pleasure ships go; you're more likely to encounter walruses than big cruise boats after this point. You'll first head southwest to Kodiak Island, which rests on the line of demarcation between coastal spruce forests around the Gulf of Alaska and the treeless Aleutian Islands, which stretch 1,200 miles into the Pacific. "Kodiak is home to giant brown bears [coastal grizzly]," West says. "If we don't encounter them here, we'll almost certainly find them in Katmai National Park at a place called Geographic Harbor. The bears come down to the water's edge to feed on mussels, and we can get close enough in the Zodiacs to hear the crunch of the shells as they chomp down. Then it's on to the Shumagin Islands, where we can walk beaches littered with petrified wood dating back twenty million years."

The stature of Alaska's mountains and glaciers and the power of its mammals certainly give visitors some perspective on their place in the world. A landing on a few of the islands in the Bering Strait further broadens that perspective. Historically, it has been important for the subsistence whale hunters of this region to live on the strait, as its narrowness forces the whales to pass fairly close to land as they migrate north and south. There are days when you're in the strait and whale spouts will be visible from the deck of the ship to the horizon. On Little Diomede, which is not much more than a steep rock in the middle of the strait, people live in little houses carved in the hillside. "The houses are on stilts; even the school gym is on stilts, as there's so little level ground," West says. "You feel as though you'd roll into the sea if you ever fell down. People live from what they can catch and kill. You'll pass houses where there are polar bear skins stretched out to dry, or walrus blubber hanging from a porch railing, melting and dripping. It's amazing to see people living in such a hostile environment. We'll visit people in their home, and they're very willing to share details about their lives. One of our guests asked the resident of the home with the walrus blubber what it was doing on the porch. 'It's aging,' he replied. 'Why?' the guest inquired. 'It tastes much better,' the man replied."

While life is hard on the Alaskan side of the Bering Strait, difficulties increase a hundredfold on the Russian side. "The Yupics on Little Diomede and Saint Lawrence Island have snow machines (what most people think of as snowmobiles), guns, and outboard motors," West reports. "There's an airport on Saint Lawrence, and some of the kids are wearing Nikes and Chicago Bulls T-shirts. But as we walk the villages of Russia's Chukchi Peninsula, it's evident that people have no modern amenities. They wear clothing made of animal skins and hunt walruses and whales with spears from walrus-skin kayaks. When we visit the villages of Provideniya and Yanrakynnot, we can walk among the huge repositories of whale skeletons that line the beach— hundreds and hundreds of them, testament to the people's subsistence life. Yet the people we encounter are very friendly and hospitable to their American visitors.

"Visiting these villagers shows that one need not have much to be happy."

2

ULTIMATE ANTARCTICA

WHY: The Southern Continent is a rare destination that offers a sense
of true wilderness, and this trip, on a smaller expedition craft, allows close
encounters with icebergs, elephant seals, and penguins.

ANTARCTICA IS THE WORLD'S LAST GREAT FRONTIER, so inhospitable to human life that there are no indigenous people on the continent—despite the fact that it encompasses more than 14 million square miles, roughly 1.5 times the size of the United States. Antarctica's isolation from civilization has permitted its natural environs to remain much as they were hundreds, if not thousands, of years ago. A trip here on a small expedition ship like the MS *Adventurer* allows total immersion in the natural world in a place where, in the words of former documentary filmmaker and adventure travel professional Barbara Banks, "people don't even factor in."

Your trip on the *Adventurer* begins with a crossing of the Drake Passage, from Cape Horn at the southern tip of Chile to the South Shetland Islands, which lie within Antarctic territory; it's considered one of the world's most precarious passages. The winds, dubbed "the Roaring Forties" and "Furious Fifties" by mariners, blow unimpeded by any landmass, and the seas can reach heights of 65 feet. Yet the 360-foot *Adventurer* handles wind and waves with great aplomb, thanks to its state-of-the-art Sperry Gyrofin stabilizers. The ship was specifically designed for ice cruising, which allows for safe exploration of narrow channels and bays that are often inaccessible to larger vessels within Antarctic waters. Comfort is not compromised for safety. All staterooms face outside and include an en suite bathroom, a music system, and individual temperature controls. The *Adventurer* accommodates just 112 passengers and boasts ample public space, including two spacious lounges, a window-lined dining room, and a well-stocked library.

"When you wake up the morning after departing from Ushuaia, Argentina, you're well across the passage," Banks explains. "The ship has an open bridge policy, so you can ride up with the

The MS Adventurer, *designed for ice cruising, can bring guests closer than any other vessel to Antarctica's wonders.*

Colonies of hundreds of thousands of penguins create an almost deafening din.

captain. The amount of instrumentation is overwhelming; being up on the bridge gives you perspective on how deeply the captain must concentrate, even though all you see is open water. You're pretty far north of the Antarctic Peninsula when the first icebergs come into view. Even though everyone has seen pictures or film footage of icebergs, you're not prepared for your first one, the enormity of them. They're like large airplanes."

The *Adventurer* is outfitted to help guests spend as much time on shore as possible. A small armada of Zodiacs are on call to spirit guests to seal colonies, abandoned whaling stations, and, at one point early in the trip, a swimming hole. "There's a place called Neptune's Bellows that we access by Zodiac where there are vents in the ocean floor where heat from the geothermic activity below seeps out," Banks explains. "The swimming area is pretty limited—one step in the wrong direction, and you're either in very hot or very cold water. It's an odd sensation—you're in the midst of this white continent of ice and snow, but you're reminded that it was born of fire."

Many landings bring visitors face-to-face with the animals of Antarctica, including large colonies of elephant seals. These are the largest member of the pinniped family, with males in the Southern Hemisphere reaching a length of 18 feet and a weight of more than 5,000 pounds. Elephant seals are easily recognized by their size and prominent proboscis; the males' fighting behavior during mating season has been frequently featured in nature documentaries. "The animals are everywhere, snorting, snuffling, digging themselves in the sand, and you have to thread your way through a maze of them, often within a foot of them," Banks says. "The colonies of king penguins are almost beyond belief, literally hundreds of thousands of birds, as far as you can see along the shore. The din as you get off the Zodiacs is almost deafening. The parents take turns fishing to get food for their young. The only way they have to find their young among the legions of birds is by voice. The smell is something else you're not quite prepared for. It's—well, strong!"

Visitors might expect to be under the close scrutiny of their naturalist guides whenever they leave the boat, but that isn't the case. When Zodiacs make their first landing, guests are given a short briefing. The gist of it is, "The Zodiacs will return here at two-thirty and will run back and forth to the ship until four. Please be here." "I didn't expect to be able to walk off on my own to explore," Banks says. "To be able to experience this remote place by yourself strikes home the grandeur of this larger-than-life landscape." Not that guests are left to fend for themselves on the Lost Continent. On the *Adventurer*, they receive in-depth lectures on the Antarctica's fauna and ample safety briefings. And if they choose to stay near their assigned naturalist, they may The lectures in themselves are like a crash course in marine biology and have included such notable scientists at Rick Price, a marine biologist for the British Antarctic Survey who has worked on nature documentaries (*The Life of Birds* and *Life in the Freezer*) with Sir David Attenborough.

The guests on the *Adventurer* might get a small taste of what it may have been like for past travelers (like famed explorer Ernest Shackleton) to have the ice close about their ship; to reach an old British research station, the captain drives the ship up onto the ice. "The boat was in a bay filled with floating ice, and there was some stationary ice before us," Banks recalls. "The captain gunned the engine, and we plowed through the pack ice and came to a rest. Suddenly, everything was deathly still. The motion we'd become used to just stopped. The crew put down the gangplank, and the captain announced that we could follow the flags in the ice to the old station. Dating from the 1940s, it lacked heat and comforts of any kind. There were still old food tins on the shelves. Wildlife researchers still use the shack, despite its utter lack of amenities. Visiting that little shack gave me a sense of humankind's incredible capacity to carve a home out in even the most desolate wilderness."

3

EXTREME FLY-FISHING IN THE CHILEAN FJORDS

WHY: The luxurious *Atmosphere* delivers you to seldom—if ever—fished trout
streams among the glaciers of southern Chile.

SINCE OUTDOOR WRITERS LIKE THE LATE ERNEST SCHWIEBERT discovered the
angling possibilities of Patagonia in the early 1960s, countless fly fishers have longed to trek
south to revel in some of the finest trout fishing in the world. Patagonian anglers generally visit
one of a host of large guest ranches where they have access to several streams on the property
and are treated to a taste of estancia life. Very nice and civilized—but what if you were to take
the angler off the estancia and put her on a luxury ship that's outfitted to reach rivers and lakes
up and down the southern coast of Chile, rivers and lakes that might have never seen a fisher-
man or artificial fly?

That's exactly what international adventure angler and professional photographer Brian
O'Keefe experienced when he set foot on board the *Atmosphere,* the mother ship of an expedition outfit called Nomads of the Seas.

Using air, land, and water, Nomads of the Seas has designed a fishing transportation system
that is unique—and has created a high-end fly-fishing experience that's second to none. The
first thing that catches your eye is the bright red Bell 407 helicopter on the back deck—imagine
a Ferrari that can fly at 150 miles per hour, carry six anglers and guides, and land on mountain-
tops, beaches, and gravel bars. (Nomads founder/owner Andrés Ergas flew helicopters in an
earlier life while serving in the Chilean army.) There are boats for every possible piscatorial assault, including five 20-foot, 200-horsepower inboard jet boats so angling teams can reach different rivers, a 24-foot 450-horsepower ten-passenger jet boat for larger groups, a 33-foot Zodiac
that can reach speeds of 50 miles per hour for whale watching—plus some smaller Zodiacs for
fly-in fishing. There's also a gourmet kitchen, a whale-watching platform, a sauna, an on-deck
spa with four hot tubs (from which you can see the whales), and a masseuse. "I don't think anyone has ever invested so much in a fishing operation," Brian O'Keefe says. "The scenery and the
quality of the fishing are enough to make this a remarkable trip, but to have so many comforts
at your disposal on a fishing boat is unheard-of."

Adventurers join the *Atmosphere* at Puerto Montt, which is reached by plane via a ninety-

Lunker brown trout await anglers on the Atmosphere. *Trout were introduced to the waters of Chile and Argentina at the turn of the last century.*

minute flight from Santiago. Over the course of a fishing week, the boat travels 400 miles along the central and southern coast of Chile, past glaciers, around fjords, and in the shadow of the towering mountains and volcanoes of the southern Andes. (San Valentín, at the southern end of the excursion, reaches a dizzying 13,000 feet above sea level—especially dizzying when you consider that you're viewing it *from* sea level.) Patagonia's 250 million acres remain largely unsettled by humans and quite unexplored. That's part of the thrill of this voyage—the chance to walk and fish waters where few if any others have trod.

Your guides on the *Atmosphere* are all seasoned fly fishers, equally ready to help beginners perfect their fly cast or lead experienced anglers to bigger fish. They work closely with the crew to keep the fishing experiences fresh. "Some days, we lowered the jet boats and sped up unnamed rivers to chase brown and rainbow trout," O'Keefe says. "One day, we helicoptered into a river where the Nomads team had a few McKenzie drift boats secreted away, and we jumped into the boat with our guide and drifted downstream, to be picked up later by the Bell. The water was so clear, you could see big trout coming out from behind submerged logs to take the fly. Another day, we took the copter into a lake and fished it and some of the creeks that fed in.

The coast of southern Chile is carved with innumerable glaciers, rivers, and lakes that have never been fished.

It's a great mix of fishing—casting attractor patterns on the feeder creeks, drifting nymphs on pocket water in small streams, throwing streamers on the bigger rivers. The two constants are that the scenery is mind-bogglingly beautiful and the fish, on average, quite large. Flying in the helicopter is incredibly cool—you fly through the fjords, over glaciers, and past waterfalls. With all the fisheries available, and all the different means to get to the rivers and lakes, it's going to take Andrés and company years to figure out all the possibilities."

Oversized trout (and the occasional steelhead, silver, and king salmon) are not the only fauna you'll encounter along the Chilean fjords. These waters are home to a number of cetacean species, including Peale's, dusky, and black dolphins and beaked, sperm, killer, and blue whales—the latter being the largest animal in the world. Wandering albatrosses will often follow the ship for much of its course, displaying their ten-plus-foot wingspans as if in salute. "I saw my first penguin as we approached one of the beaches," O'Keefe recalls, "and passed colonies of hundreds of seals. The abundance of animal life is astounding."

The experience of traveling and fishing on the *Atmosphere* is perhaps best captured by the setting of a luncheon O'Keefe enjoyed after a productive morning on the river. "It had been a rainy morning—as is often the case in Patagonia—but we'd enjoyed some excellent fishing. As we waited for the helicopter, our guides made a fire to keep us warm. Once the helicopter arrived, we boarded and headed back toward the mother ship. We couldn't see the mountains for the clouds, but eventually we popped out. As we approached the ship, Andrés suddenly veered the Bell away. Soon after, we landed on a glacier. There were several canopies set up to shelter tables that were laid out with sliced meats, cheeses, bread, various Chilean wines, scotch, and a pitcher of pisco sours—the unofficial national cocktail of Chile. One of the crew members was coming down the glacier with crampons and an ice ax and a bag of blue ice that he'd scraped from the glacier—maybe ten thousand years old? He proceeded to mash up the ice and make us drinks, which we sipped while taking in the waterfalls and glaciers around us."

4

EXPLORING THE GALÁPAGOS

WHY: Experience the incongruous, exotic assemblage of wildlife—nearly
tame—around the islands that inspired Darwin's masterwork,
On the Origin of Species.

MENTION THE GALÁPAGOS, AND MANY IMAGES SPRING TO mind: giant tortoises, sea lions, penguins, iguanas, flamingoes. As in Charles Darwin's time, the great attraction of the Galapágos is the odd and wonderful assemblage of fauna that call the islands home—and how readily accessible these animals are. "In our day-to-day lives, most of us don't have much interaction with wildlife," says Bill Abbott, an adventure travel pioneer and the founder of Wilderness Travel who was raised in Venezuela and Brazil. "But in the Galápagos you do—and you get very close to the animals, often within a few feet. I've been to the Galápagos seven times now, and I know what to expect, yet every time I go, I come away awed."

Visitors generally take in the Galapágos by boat. "We use three-masted motorsailers," Abbott says, "which provide a romantic ambiance for our sixteen guests, especially when the sails are flying. It reinforces the idea that you're following in the wake of Darwin." Each day is a mix of hikes and snorkeling excursions, with a little time in between for relaxing on board and taking in the scenery from the deck. Guest berths are air-conditioned and include en suite bathrooms. The menu mixes comfort foods like pastas (great after an active day outdoors) with lighter fare (salads, light soups, and fresh fish) and offers ample vegetarian options. All the food is freshly prepared, and almost every meal is finished off with a huge platter of fresh fruits—sliced melon, mango, and pineapple. The limited number of guests makes the logistics for shore landings very easy to manage.

The Galápagos archipelago consists of sixty-one islands situated 600 miles off the coast of Ecuador. The eclectic array of animal life on these isolated islands raises the question "How did they get here . . . and why?" Scientists believe that the Galápagos were created from volcanic

Galápagos travelers split their time between nature walks and snorkeling; visitors must stay on designated trails to protect native flora.

The animals of the Galápagos have little or no fear of humans, allowing intimate interactions that are rare anywhere else.

activity on the ocean floor and that they've never been connected to a continent. All of their resident animals—including some fifty endemic terrestrial species found nowhere else in the world—arrived by swimming (seals, dolphins, penguins), floating (tortoises, iguanas, insects, some plants), or flying (birds, seeds floating in air currents) from as far afield as the Caribbean and the Antarctic. The why is a bit harder to answer, though the fact that two important ocean currents—the Southern Humboldt Current and Northern Panama Current—flow near the Galápagos certainly facilitated and influenced the passage of animal and plant life. Once there, the animals were able to adapt and survive—despite the unbalanced assortment of species—thanks to the absence of predators.

"There seems to be no end of animals," Abbott says. "At Espanola Island, we'll find large flocks of wave albatross, which land with an awkward bump and roll. They're large birds, with a wingspan of seven feet; when you're sitting, they almost come up to your head. I've watched their intricate courtship, when they click their beaks together and wave their wings." At Espanola and North Seymour Islands, you'll come upon one of the Galápagos's signature birds, the blue-footed booby. Its feet are startlingly blue, and its courtship display is both bizarre and comical.

Other land highlights include magnificent frigates, Galápagos hawks, Darwin's finches (so tame they'll land on your shoulder), and, of course, the giant tortoises (reaching weights of more than 600 pounds) for which the islands are named. The tortoises and land birds are often found on or near the islands' walking trails, which means you're seeing these animals nose-to-nose, allowing for intimate photography opportunities. (Visitors must remain on trails while traversing the islands, to minimize impact on the habitat.)

The underwater life of the Galápagos is as big an attraction as the animals on land, and Wilderness Travel's trips schedule time each day for snorkeling. On a single swim, you might see fur seals, California sea lions, and penguins. They seem as curious about humans as we are about them, and they'll swim close to observe you or follow you about. Around the island of Fernandina are large groups of marine iguanas. Sometimes you'll see them in the water, but more often they'll be sunning on the rocks. "One time I was swimming with a group off Fernandina when we came upon a large group of giant sea turtles," Abbott recalls. "There must have been twenty-five, and they kept coming and coming. At that same spot, I saw a flightless cormorant diving underwater for fish. I swam up to him, trying to figure out what he was eating. When I went up for air, the bird popped up right next to me, beak at my mask. It looked at me, then dove back down. The animals here don't see people as a threat." Visitors can also take *pangas* (motorized dinghies) across lagoons on several of the islands. Rays and sharks congregate in these lagoons, and the water is clear enough that they can be viewed from the boat.

By law, all visitors must be accompanied by naturalists certified by the Ecuadorian National Park Service. "You need someone to flip over each leaf and provide a context," Abbott says. "That's what the naturalists do. They bring in Darwin's theory, so you're not just looking at animals but gaining an understanding of a complex ecosystem." The guides become part of the larger group on these cruises; they're with you on walks, but they also enjoy cocktails with you as the sun sets over the equator, sharing stories about the animals and growing up in the Galápagos.

5

THE SPICE ISLANDS BY *PHINISI*

WHY: This one-of-a-kind traditional sailing vessel based on a centuries-old design transports you back to the days of the thriving spice trade, plying the seas of Indonesia while embracing you with modern-day comforts.

THE FIRST THING YOU NOTICE ABOUT THE *SILOLONA* is its billowing black sails. As you get closer, you realize that they are not an omen of evil but a sign that very good things are about to be bestowed upon you.

"The *Silolona* is the Indonesian answer to the great white yacht of the Mediterranean," Sonia Burdin, who is a veteran of the luxury-travel industry, declares. "First of all, it's completely hewn from wood—ironwood, teak, and lengua—inside and out. There's nothing glitzy or plastic about it. Second, it's built according to the ancestral techniques of the famed Konjo boatbuilders of southern Sulawesi. The basic design follows that of the *phinisi*, the traditional vessel of Indonesia, to honor its long history here—though the five guest cabins rival a five-star hotel in terms of their comfort and design."

The *Silolona* offers one of the world's most exclusive sailing charters, conveying guests (a maximum of ten) to a host of venues scattered across the waters of Southeast Asia. Some guests charter the *Silolona* to scuba dive, and the waters that the ship plies—from Raja Ampat (northwest of New Guinea) to Komodo Island National Park to the Andaman Sea (west of Thailand and Myanmar) offer some of the world's richest underwater biodiversity, from pygmy seahorses to bumphead parrotfish, amid dense stands of soft coral. Some of the *Silolona*'s itineraries are geared toward providing guests with a well-researched and highly personalized cultural or historic overview of a particular region—like a voyage to the Banda Islands and a history of the spice trade, or a chance learn about the Dani and Asmat peoples who dwell on islands off West Papua. Some charter the ship for the ideal family escape, as the crew is happy to entertain the children, taking them fishing, swimming, or exploring, so Mom and Dad can have some

The Silolona *sails to many exotic destinations, including the Komodo Islands* (opposite), *the Mergui archipelago, and the Spice Islands.*

time alone. Each of these journeys has its own special appeal, but the one constant—and perhaps the main reason to embark—is the splendor of the *Silolona* itself and the gracious service of the crew.

The *Silolona* is the first traditional *phinisi* ship built to Germanischer Lloyd standards and designed specifically for safe cruising. Owner Patti Seery's sense of design—and her understanding of its importance in creating inviting spaces—is very much in evidence on the ship. "The attention to details on the *Silolona* is outstanding," Burdin says. "Each of the suites has a style in keeping with the cultures of some of the islands we visit—Bali, Java, Asmat, Borneo, and Sumba. The Bali Suite, for example, features an ancient Kasaman painting (Kasaman is the center of the most ancient Balinese painting style), from a Hindu temple, in cream, black, and deep maroon, which gave the tone for the entire style of *Silolona*. Another fine piece of Balinese textile embellishes the cabin: a red and black double-ikat woven bed runner from Tenganan."

"The Indonesian people are the most genuine, heartwarming people I've ever met."

While regional motifs and materials are used, the comfort level is outstanding. Every cabin has a daybed, an in-room music system, air-conditioning, and a full bath with shower. The spacious lounge and dining area, all adorned in teak, is surrounded by large windows and creates an inviting space for a first coffee in the morning when everyone else is still asleep or for perusing a book about Southeast Asia from the boat's library. There's a lovely covered seating area in the back of the boat where guests can enjoy tea or cocktails when the last rays of the sun give the *Silolona*'s wood a honey tint, and ample space on the sundeck and the foredeck to take in the sights and sun. The shaded alfresco dining deck is the perfect area to enjoy a scrumptious breakfast in the sea breeze.

As fabulous as the accommodations on the *Silolona* are, Burdin believes that it's the Indonesian crew that makes the sail truly memorable. "The Indonesian people are the most genuine, heartwarming people I've ever met," she says. "They have wonderful smiles, and their style of service is discreet and very sincere; there's no obsequiousness." There are seventeen crew members on the *Silolona* for the ten passengers. Whether it's greeting passengers with cooled, lemongrass-scented towels, picking native fruits and concocting smoothies for a midafternoon repast, or helping you catch some fresh fish for dinner, the crew is always at your disposal.

"There's also a five-star chef on board," Burdin adds. "While he likes to prepare Indonesian foods and Asian fusion to heighten the experience of the area, he can do anything—from five-course continental meals to an omelet. Guests are interviewed before the trip so any food dislikes, allergies, or favorite dishes are taken into consideration for the excursion's journey menu."

Sonia Burdin's adventure on the *Silolona* sought to shed light on the spice trade. "We headed from Ambon to the Banda Islands, which with the nearby Moluccas were once the world's only source for nutmeg," Burdin says. "In the sixteenth and seventeenth centuries, nutmeg was worth more than gold, and the British and Dutch battled over the islands. Many people don't realize that the Dutch conceded New Amsterdam to the British in exchange for the Brits' relinquishment of claims to the Bandas. When the *Silolona* arrived at Banda Neira [the administrative capital], it felt like we had sailed back into Jacobean times. Twenty men came paddling out in two *kora koras,* traditional canoes that are very long and thin, with drums beating. There's a little fishing village at water level and, on the hillside, the Dutch fort Belgica. In between there's a mosque. When we got to shore, throngs of people gathered around us. They had biscuits with nutmeg jam waiting."

The *Silolona* is sailed today much as *phinisi* were sailed hundreds of years ago, and you'll want to rise early at least one morning to watch the crew hoist her sails. "When I stirred at sunrise, the crew had donned their sarongs and matching head scarves in traditional patterns from their villages," Burdin recalls. "They were climbing about the masts, agile and supremely confident, as Nasir, who oversees the men, called out orders. In the background, the sun was coming over the stark volcanic mountains of Banda, reflecting off a glassy sea."

6

Melanesia: Swimming with Mantas, Dancing with Fire

WHY: Immerse yourself in the remote western Pacific cultures of Papua New Guinea and revel in treasured ocean experiences—swimming with manta rays off the island of Yap and among the jellyfish of Palau—on the *Clipper Odyssey*.

M ELANESIA AND MICRONESIA — ROUGHLY SPEAKING, the myriad islands that fan out around the eastern edge of Papua New Guinea and the region also known as the Caroline Islands—are among the least traveled and most tantalizing corners of the far western Pacific. Those who make the journey get to experience both anthropological wonders in the shape of thriving indigenous cultures and some of the Pacific's richest and most diverse marine life.

"These are places where there are no airports, many of the women do not wear tops, some islands don't allow motors, and the catch of the day is the thing to be proud of," Jack Grove, a marine biologist and professional naturalist, who travels and lectures about the world's oceans, explains. "The white-sand beaches with no footprints, adorned by coconut trees and fringed by azure seas alive with healthy coral reefs certainly contribute to the appeal of this trip. But what makes this trip special to me is the chance guests have to immerse themselves in the values of these places. We've gotten to know the people over the last twenty years, and they're very happy to share elements of their culture with outsiders who are respectful. There's good reason to go soon—global climate change poses a great threat to the low-lying atolls of Micronesia, and in coming decades they could very well slip into the sea."

The *Clipper Odyssey* will be your home as you cruise the western Pacific for 2,500 miles, visiting some seventeen islands and atolls over two weeks as you move from Port Moresby in southeastern Papua New Guinea to Palau, your terminus in the west. The vessel has five decks, complete with an outdoor pool, a library, several lounges, a gym, and even a jogging track. Din-

A paddle dancer in the Trobriand Islands, a regular stop on the Clipper Odyssey's *tour of Melanesia.*

ners are prepared individually, with an emphasis on fresh fish. You'll also have a chance to sample local produce—coconuts, yams, breadfruit, taro, and cassava.

The ship embarks from Port Moresby, cruising east in the shadow of the soaring Owen Stanley Range, which shoots from near sea level to elevations of 13,000 feet. An early exclamation point comes on your second day at sea, as you arrive in the Trobriand Islands. Sarong-clad Kitava islanders raise the sails on elaborate *kula* canoes—each carved from a single log and decorated with mother-of-pearl and fresh hibiscus—and sail out to meet the ship. When you reach shore, the greeting continues with a series of ceremonial dances. These include the "tapioca" dance, generally performed only during the island's yam harvest. Continuing uphill to the village of Kumwageya, you'll have a chance to peruse the intricate wood carvings

> "It can be an eerie experience when a manta swims overhead, as it blocks out the sun."

of Trobriand master craftsmen—bowls, human and animal figures, walking sticks—polished to a sheen by pig tusks and considered some of the best Melanesia has to offer.

Several days later, the fire dances of the Baining tribe on the island of New Britain are another cultural highlight. You approach the island via the harbor of Rabaul, a flooded caldera on the north end that's dramatically ringed by six cone-shaped volcanoes; a few are still active, sometimes belching plumes of steam. The fire dances, which honor local spirits, are conducted at night. "The tribesmen slap sections of bamboo of different lengths and girths with rubber flip-flops," Grove explains, "producing a mesmerizing, thud-like sound in a variety of pitches that crescendoes as the dance unfolds. The dancers spray their skin with a coconut-based fluid, which gives it a sooty appearance, and don huge masks—some more than six feet in height—made of local fibers, and penis sheaths. They don't walk on hot coals; they stomp, with flames and sparks rising above their shoulders. The cacophony of the bamboo drums, the chanting of the performers, the flames dancing against the darkness—it's completely hypnotic."

There's an opportunity (or two) every day to snorkel—or, if you're certified, dive. (The *Clipper Odyssey* is outfitted to serve scuba divers, and there are several qualified dive masters aboard; however, the number of diving guests on board on any given expedition is limited. All snorkeling gear is provided; weights and tanks are available for divers.) "Every place we stop, you can hop into a Zodiac, motor a few minutes to a reef, and slide over the side to find a kaleidoscope of colorful fishes and corals," Grove says. "In one spot, we might come upon a gigantic green Napoleon wrasse, which can reach over six feet and four hundred pounds. In another, brilliant schooling species like anthias and damselfishes." The *Clipper Odyssey*'s talented team of naturalists—including Jack Grove—accompany every snorkel and dive, helping you locate interesting species and place what you've just seen into the context of the reef's ecosystem.

If there's one animal that many scuba divers and snorkelers long to interact with, it's the manta ray. The largest member of the ray family, mantas can reach lengths of 12 feet, widths of nearly 20 feet, and weights approaching 5,000 pounds. Despite their tremendous size they are extremely docile creatures, gliding effortlessly through the water and subsisting on plankton and small fish, which they direct into their expansive mouths with their distinctive "horns." The waters off the four islands of Yap are one of the most reliable regions in the world to encounter mantas. "Encounters are so common that individual animals can be recognized by the combination of markings on the back and belly, and local people have given them names," Grove says. "If you're scuba diving, it can be an eerie experience when a manta swims overhead, as it blocks out the sun." Manta rays are often curious about humans and will glide close to have a look at you with their grapefruit-sized eyes.

The excursion ends in the Republic of Palau, a collection of more than two hundred islands on the southern edge of the Philippine Sea. Palau gained some mainstream notoriety as the site of the 2005 installment of the reality-television saga *Survivor,* but the scuba diving community has recognized the bounties of its extensive barrier reefs—some 1,300 fish species—for many years. A one-of-a-kind snorkeling experience awaits you after a short hike inland on the island of Eli Malk, at Jellyfish Lake. Eons ago, moon and mestiga jellyfish were trapped when a submerged reef rose, cutting the saltwater lake off from the ocean. As these jellies face no predators in their sanctum, they've evolved to the point where they no longer have the ability to sting; they're sustained by algae that resides within their cells. Each day, the jellyfish swim from one side of the lake to the other to absorb sunlight to foster algae growth. After a steep but brief climb up a forested trail, you'll come out upon the brilliant blue lake and its ethereal denizens flitting just below the surface. "I find the experience sensual, and that's not a word I use often," Grove says. "This is one place I encourage guests not to wear any type of Lycra suit so that the globular, pulsating invertebrates come in direct contact with the skin. It's a remarkable tactile experience—and, if your mind is receptive, a spiritual one."

7

MEXICO: SWIMMING WITH GREAT WHITE SHARKS

WHY: Cage diving off Mexico's Isla Guadalupe allows you to go
eye-to-eye with the ocean's apex predator in complete safety,
even if you're not a certified diver.

M OST OCEAN SWIMMERS WOULD PREFER *NOT* TO COME into contact with great white sharks. Yet the chance to swim with these powerful, potentially man-eating fish poses the ultimate thrill, an opportunity to gain a firsthand understanding of the habits of this near-mythic creature. Operators in South Africa and Australia once had a monopoly on great-white-shark diving, thanks to reliable numbers of animals there. But a few years back, a new great-white-shark diving locale was discovered off the coast of Baja California. "I began hearing reports from tuna fishermen who were encountering large numbers of great white sharks off Isla Guadalupe, an isolated island about two hundred miles southwest of San Diego," says Patric Douglas, founder of Shark Diver, which has been featured on the National Geographic and Discovery channels. "I accompanied a group down there, and we dropped a shark cage into the water. Two hours later, there were four great whites around us."

Your rendezvous with Isla Guadalupe's great white sharks begins with a twenty-four-hour ocean crossing from San Diego on one of the vessels operated by Shark Diver—the MV *Islander* or the MV *Horizon*. The ships were designed for long-range marine research and scuba diving expeditions; while not luxurious, they offer essential creature comforts. Each of the staterooms is air-conditioned and outfitted with two single beds and a washbasin; guests share bathrooms equipped with hot showers. The galley/salon area can accommodate everyone at mealtimes (a maximum of sixteen guests per trip); it includes an entertainment center so you can watch any video footage of the day's diving that your fellow guests might have captured. Guests like to unwind here between dives, or on the ships' ample sundecks. Dinner is imaginative and well

More than 120 different great white sharks have been identified off Isla Guadalupe—all from the safety of shark-proof cages.

prepared; one favorite entrée is fresh yellowfin tuna (cut 1 to 2 inches thick) marinated in light seaweed soy sauce, dipped in toasted sesame seeds, seared, and served on wasabi mashed potatoes, with a small seaweed salad.

Though the crossing can occasionally be a bit rough, the waters around Isla Guadalupe are calm, belying the potential mayhem below the lapping waves. "We cross to the island at night, arriving shortly after dawn," Douglas says. "Guests wake up to a breakfast of eggs Benedict. As the plates are cleared from the table, the shark cages are being dropped in the water. By 8 A.M. the pools are open, and the sharks are generally beginning to arrive." Given the morning's coming events, you may not need that second or third cup of coffee to get your heart pumping!

The "pools" Douglas references are the cages that make swimming with sharks possible. The 20 × 20 × 15-foot cages are constructed of 1 × 1-inch aluminum bars, with a crush strength of 5,000 pounds; they're built to withstand the impact of a curious great white that decides to try to get a closer look at you, and they offer 360-degree visibility. "Scent" (fish guts and blood) is released into the water to help draw the animals in, though often the sound of the cages being lowered into the water is enough to attract their attention. After sliding into a 5-millimeter-thick wet suit to ensure your comfort in the 68-degree Fahrenheit water, you'll don

"When the shark's eye locks on you, everything else in the world disappears."

your mask and air-supply hose, step to the boat's diving platform, and ease into one of the two cages that rest at water level, attached to the boat. (Since your oxygen is supplied from the boat, you don't need dive certification to swim with the sharks, though some diving experience might enhance your comfort underwater.) Each cage can accommodate four to five divers, and dives tend to last an hour. With the cages open ten hours a day, you can log up to five dives a day—or more, if your fellow divers choose to spend less time in the water.

Exhilarating is not too strong a word for a first encounter with a great white shark. "On my first white-shark dive, the crew advised me not to dawdle on the platform that you step on to access the diving cage, as the sharks will sometimes come up onto it," recalls Ethan Gordon, an accomplished underwater photographer and scuba journalist. "My heart was pounding as I envisioned a fifteen-foot shark coming up onto the platform. I spend a lot of time in the water, and there simply aren't many things that you come in contact with that are so big as a great white. When you stare through the bottom of the cage and the shark seems as wide as the cage itself, you have the sense that if it wants to come in, it can—though statistically speaking, this is not going to happen. Still, years of evolutionary instinct kick in, and you definitely feel a flight instinct. That's a big part of the thrill.

"Even though the visibility can be a hundred feet, most of the time you don't see the sharks until they're almost upon the cage," Gordon says. "You think you see a shadow down in the deep, but usually it's your eyes playing tricks on you. Just as your attention begins to slip away, you see a movement out of the corner of your eye and a shark is approaching the cage at top speed." Douglas and his crew have identified more than 120 separate white sharks at Isla Guadalupe. It's not uncommon to have several sharks visiting the cages at one time. Crew members can identify specimens by both physical characteristics and behaviors. Some have earned nicknames; there's Starboard, a female that has big scars along her right side, and Shredder, who once shredded a thick anchor rope. There's also Fat Tony, who earned his moniker from his bullying, mafioso-like ways.

"Fat Tony likes to hit the cage from the bottom," Douglas explains. "We don't know for certain why he does this, but we believe that he understands that the creatures inside the cage are capable of responding to his action, and he's looking for a reaction." While some sharks don't seem to take any interest in the divers in the cage, others do. Even spookier, there are times when a shark seems to focus on a particular diver. No one is quite prepared for this. The shark's eyeball can rotate; when it locks on an individual, it can stay focused on that diver even as the shark swims past until the eye is almost halfway around in its socket.

"When the eye locks on you, everything else in the world disappears—it's just you and that shark," Douglas explains. "It's a chilling feeling when a predator as fearsome as a great white shark is that close and has taken an interest in you. Most of our clients are not used to having predators eye *them*. I think the experience puts your existence as a human in perspective. You realize that here in the middle of the Pacific, you're not necessarily at the top of the food chain."

8

DIVING TO THE *TITANIC* OFF NEWFOUNDLAND

WHY: Be one of very few to see the *Titanic* at its final resting place,
at a depth of more than 12,000 feet, gaining new perspective on one
of the last century's greatest maritime tragedies.

OF THE MANY LITERARY EFFORTS REFLECTING UPON THE sinking of the *Titanic*, Thomas Hardy's "The Convergence of the Twain" is perhaps the most haunting:

> *And as the smart ship grew*
> *In stature, grace, and hue*
> *In shadowy silent distance grew the Iceberg too.*
>
> *Alien they seemed to be:*
> *No mortal eye could see*
> *The intimate welding of their later history.*

Whether you embrace Hardy's fatalistic view of the ship's demise or see it as divine retribution for the transgressions of human pride (the ship had been proclaimed "unsinkable"), the *Titanic* has held the world's imagination for nearly a century—though for much of that period its exact whereabouts remained unknown. In 1985 the wreck of the *Titanic* was discovered lying in international waters 380 miles southeast of Newfoundland. You can venture the 12,465 feet down to the *Titanic* on one of the world's few deep-diving submersibles and contemplate first-hand some of the questions its sinking has posed.

On your adventure to the *Titanic*, you'll be joining the crew of the research ship RV *Akademik Mstislav Keldysh* as part of a research mission that's partially sponsored by the Moscow-based Shirshov Institute of Oceanology. The *Keldysh* was designed specifically to support deep-dive expeditions and includes seventeen laboratories and a specialized library covering underwater

Visitors to the Titanic *can view many details of the ship. This is the* Titanic's *telemotor, the main control unit on the bridge. The wheel has rotted away, and various plaques have been left, placed by the submersible's manipulator.*

archaeology, oceanography, and deep-sea exploration. Since its construction in 1981, the *Keldysh* has made nearly twenty trips to the *Titanic* and has supported more than one hundred dives. Since the vessel is primarily used for research, its cabins are not extravagant but are comfortable enough, with en suite bathrooms. It also boasts a gym, a volleyball court, and a small outdoor swimming pool. Meals are taken in a guest dining room (the ship's crew has separate dining quarters) and are prepared by professional chefs.

The two-week adventure begins in Saint John's, the provincial capital of Newfoundland and Labrador, where the *Keldysh* will pick up passengers. From here it's a two-day passage to the *Titanic*'s resting spot. En route, numerous lectures are given about the construction of the *Titanic,* the conditions that led to its demise, and the efforts to locate and explore it. By the time you get to the site, you thoroughly understand the ship's history. "Being there in the darkness and fog right where the accident happened allows guests to come to terms with the tragedy on a deeper level," deep-sea adventurer Rob McCallum explains. "You get an understanding of how unforgiving the Atlantic can be."

In 1912 the *Titanic* was the largest passenger steamship that had ever been launched and was considered one of the most technologically advanced, with electricity throughout, heated rooms, and two wireless radios for sending telegrams. The ship held the promise of not only a fast passage across the Atlantic but a luxurious one. It featured the first swimming pool (heated) on a ship, as well as a Turkish bath, gymnasium, squash court, and two barbershops.

In terms of engineering wonders, the two submersibles—*Mir 1* and *Mir 2*—rival the *Titanic*. "Climbing into the sub is a bit like boarding a hatchback car," McCallum explains. "Small, but not uncomfortably so." There are three people in the submersible—the pilot and two guests. Once you're in and the doors are secured, the sub is lowered into the water and you begin a controlled descent—roughly 100 feet per minute. It takes two hours to reach the bottom, as you're descending 12,000 feet. It's hard to imagine such a distance. (Next time you're flying and the pilot announces your altitude, look out the window and you'll get a sense of what that means.) The first 400 feet, there's light, and you can make out various creatures—jellyfish, some pelagic fish. "A colleague of mine described it well," McCallum says. " 'I pictured the ocean as water,' he said. 'In reality, it's more like minestrone soup, filled with different ingredients of life.' " By the time you reach a depth of 600 feet, visibility is getting pretty gloomy. At 1,000 feet, you've lost sunlight. It's dark for the remainder of the journey, as the sub conserves power for when you reach the bottom; navigation is by sonar.

When you finally reach the bottom, all is dark—then the pilot hits the lights, and there before you is the bow of the *Titanic*. Even guests who have studied the *Titanic* for years are taken

The submersibles of the Keldysh—Mir 1 and Mir 2—are two of only five submersibles in the world that can reach the 12,000-foot depth where the Titanic rests.

aback by its magnitude. Visibility from the submersible is only looking forward, and from this perspective, you feel small and vulnerable. Guests generally spend at least six hours on the bottom with the *Titanic,* circling it from a distance, both for safety and out of respect. The bow of the ship is in the best condition. Here winches, bollards, anchors, and anchor chains are clearly visible. The stern, which was sheared off when the boat hit bottom, rests several hundred yards behind the rest of the wreck and is badly deteriorated. (Oceanologists believe that the ship's intact structures may collapse within fifty or a hundred years, thanks to marine organisms and human contact.) Though the center section is badly twisted, you can make out where the ship's grand staircase once stood; hovering above the void, you can peer down seven stories into the ship's center. Many portholes and windows still have their glass. Near the section of the ship where the officers' quarters were housed, a white bathtub is visible through the ship's decaying walls. Sometimes you'll even catch a glimpse of a bag or shoe.

"For some, six hours is plenty of time to view the *Titanic,*" McCallum says. "Others would stay down there for weeks if they could."

ON AN ISLAND

THE TROPICAL ISLAND IDYLL HAS ENDURING APPEAL FOR TRAVELERS — ESPECIALLY IF THE GIVEN TRAVELER RESIDES IN CHICAGO AND IT'S mid-February. Although the island trips presented here *all* involve generous amounts of sun and sand, they go beyond lounging in the shade of a thatched hut and engage the voyager in the history and ecology of her surroundings.

Walk among the mysterious *moai* of Rapa Nui (Easter Island), paddle in a kayak around Moorea (considered by some to be the world's most beautiful island), learn to surf on the Indonesian island of Sumba, and experience the solitude of a few of the Seychelles' most private islands (alone, that is, except for the company of giant tortoises). No one will lack for comforts at these island retreats, as they feature some of the finest accommodations available.

Between activities, you may even find time for a midday nap in the thatched hut that just a few days before you had dreamed about in a midwinter reverie.

Another day in the Seychelles.

9

AMONG THE *MOAI* ON EASTER ISLAND

WHY: Isolated Easter Island and its mysterious monoliths have captured travelers' imaginations for generations; a luxurious new eco-lodge from Explora makes one of the world's most remote and rugged locations comfortable and even more appealing.

THERE ARE FEW ICONS SO EMBLEMATIC OF A PLACE as the great carved-stone visages—the *moai*—of Easter Island. While many schoolchildren can identify the stoic-faced totems and their home, few adults can say exactly where Easter Island (Rapa Nui in local parlance) is. The short answer to that question is "Far away." The longer answer is, some 2,200 miles (or a five-hour plane ride) west of the central coast of Chile and 1,100 miles from the nearest inhabited landmass, Pitcairn Island. By some criteria, this makes Rapa Nui the most isolated settlement in the world—yet people still make the sojourn here to walk among the *moai*.

"Though it's Chilean territory, the people of Rapa Nui have little connection with this nation or South America, for that matter," explains Josef Stirnimann, who's spent much of his career in the travel industry in South America. "Their ancestors hail from Polynesia, and their forebears are proud of their heritage. The details of that history are somewhat vague. There's no written account, just stories told from one generation to the next. Not everyone you speak with tells exactly the same story. In a way, this adds to the fascination and mystique of the place."

The first visitors to Rapa Nui are believed to have sailed from the Marquesas in French Polynesia, more than 2,000 miles, in catamarans provisioned with fowl and other foodstuffs intended for a long-term stay. They arrived around A.D. 400 and found a lush tropical island covered with millions of palm trees. By the time a Dutch ship captained by Jacob Roggeveen found harbor there in 1722, nearly all the trees were gone, harvested to build canoes and clear land for crop cultivation. Visitors thinking "South Pacific Island" may be taken aback by Rapa Nui's sweeping grasslands and rugged volcanic outcroppings that more readily suggest southern

People are dwarfed by Rapa Nui's moai, *extraordinary statues that weigh an average of fourteen tons.*

Patagonia than Tahiti. Most will agree that the island's otherworldly landscape provides a fitting backdrop for its silent stone citizens.

In upscale travel circles, the word on Easter Island has long been "It's a fascinating place—too bad there's nowhere nice to stay." This is no longer the case. Explora, which has built a reputation designing and operating deluxe lodges in out-of-the-way places like Patagonia and Atacama, has established Posada de Mike Rapu on the south of the island, overlooking the Pacific. "The architect we worked with, José Cruz Ovalle, wanted to transmit some of the designs of the Rapa Nui people into the lodge," Stirnimann says. "The roofs are shaped like boats, as in the past the island's residents would find shelter underneath their great canoes. The lodge also makes ample use of the volcanic stone that's so prevalent here. With only thirty rooms, it's intimate. Built to be respectful of its surroundings, it's already been recognized as the greenest lodge property in South America." Each of the rooms faces the east, allowing guests to take in brilliant sunrises over the Pacific. Cuisine, not surprisingly, has a local-seafood bent; tuna and swordfish caught off the island in the morning find their way to the menu at night.

Visitor activities at Rapa Nui center on exploration of the island's cultural legacy and harken back to the *moai*. There are 887 *moai* scattered around the island, each one hand-carved from a single piece of stone made of compressed volcanic ash. Some stand on ceremonial stone platforms, called *ahus;* others lie on their sides along trails, seemingly abandoned in mid-delivery. Ethnologists and archaeologists have puzzled for generations over the role the *moai* played in the life of Rapa Nui's inhabitants. Some believe they were a vehicle for communicating with the gods, others that they were tributes to tribal leaders. The form of the *moai* is sometimes mistaken for a disembodied head because many have been partially buried over the centuries and only the elongated heads remain above ground. The most striking sites are those where *moai* stand in groups. Among those are Ahu Tongariki, which includes fifteen figures, and Ahu Akivi, where seven *moai* keep vigil. Interestingly, the sentinels at Ahu Akivi are the only figures that face the water. One explanation for their positioning is that "the Seven," as they're sometimes called, represent the seven explorers who discovered the island.

Essential to the Explora program are daily hikes with bilingual local guides that allow guests to experience all the grandeur of the *moai*. Most hikes are between 3 and 9 miles and involve little elevation gain. As you walk among the island's rolling green hills en route to a *moai* site, you pass *monavais,* stone greenhouses used to grow bananas, mangoes, and avocados. Almost every-where you look you'll see wild horses. With a population of about ten thousand, they outnum-ber the human population by at least two to one, and you come upon them near the *moai*, along the ocean, in town, and even outside your window at night.

A favorite hike is Ara O Te Moai, or the Moai Route. "This walk leads to the quarry area at Rano Raraku, which has been dubbed 'the Factory' by our guides," Stirnimann says. "All the *moai* were carved here using rock tools, and all those that were carried to resting spots on other parts of the island came along this path. There are many *moai* along the trail in, and hundreds at the quarry, some not quite finished. You have the sense that scores of people were working on these gigantic statues and then one day just quit." Why nearly half of the *moai* never left the Factory is another mystery—Were they intended to remain here, or did the islanders merely run out of energy or the means to convey them? It's mind-boggling to imagine moving the largest of the *moai* in the shadow of Rano Raraku; nicknamed "El Gigante," this figure is nearly 72 feet tall, and its weight is estimated at more than 145 tons. (There's some question as to whether some of the trees that were felled were harvested for use as rollers or sleds to move the *moai,* which have an average weight of 14 tons, around the island; some Rapa Nuans insist that the *moai* were transported via spiritual power.)

Guests usually hike in the morning and enjoy a picnic lunch on an overlook above the ocean. Lodge employees will have a table set with a checkered tablecloth and comfortable folding chairs. Fare includes fresh fish and meat, hot soup, salads, desserts and wine, hot coffee and tea. As you dine, you hear the waves crashing below. Several of the nine hiking options end on Rapa Nui's two beaches, Anakena and Ovahe. A swim in the turquoise water is refreshing after the morning's walk, and your guides have snorkel gear at the ready. Guests also have the option of surfing—Explora has three boards available for guests—though the breaks are not well suited for beginners. If you're not quite ready to surf, it can be fun to watch the guides hit the breaks, as they are very talented.

10

PADDLING POLYNESIA

WHY: The bounties of Moorea, one of the world's most beautiful islands,
can be seen up close while enjoying world-class kayaking.

I F YOU'RE AT ALL INTERESTED IN TROPICAL ISLANDS, Moorea (11 miles west of
Tahiti) is one of the most spectacular you'll ever find. Many island aficionados rank nearby
Bora-Bora very high on their favorites list, but because it's older, not much of the original island
is left. Moorea is relatively young in geologic terms, and its rugged volcanic peaks are still intact.
They provide an incredible skyline, especially when viewed from the water. "If you follow the
shoreline of Moorea, its circumference is forty-four miles—just the right size to explore in a
week by kayak," says Frank Murphy, a longtime marine researcher on the island. "Moorea is
kayak-friendly because it's surrounded by a coral reef that shields the shoreline from the surf.
Virtually all of your paddling is in a warm, protected lagoon that's eight to ten feet deep, over a
substratum that's covered with colorful corals that are changing shades all day as the sun moves
through the sky."

Frank Murphy's paddle tour of Moorea begins from the Pearl Resort and Spa on the north-
eastern edge of the island and heads counterclockwise, putting the trade winds at your back.
"We turn into Cook's Bay the first morning for the first of many breathtaking views, looking
back at the interior of the valley with its jagged peaks," Murphy explains. "Even though this area
has more structures than most of the island, the homes and small hotels on stilts above the water don't distract from the beauty of the mountains." You'll stop for lunch at a beach farther
west, where there's some excellent snorkeling and a good chance to swim with sea turtles. From
here it's a short paddle to your evening's lodging, the family-run Tarariki Village. Tarariki has
open-air thatched bungalows, each with a separate bathroom, set in gardens of native flora up
against the beach. The first day's schedule sets the pattern for the week: paddle in the morning,
explore, swim, snorkel, or relax in the afternoon.

The next day, the group paddles into Opunohu Bay, where Captain James Cook moored on
his visit to Moorea in 1769. (Opunohu was featured in the 1984 blockbuster *The Bounty*.) "We

Most guest accommodations on Moorea are near the water—or literally on the water!

cover the history of the bay, the ramifications of European discovery for Moorea, and the ecological significance of the valley in the distance—a valley we'll hike through later," Murphy says. "We'll stop in the village of Papetoai, site of the oldest Christian church in French Polynesia, and discuss the history of missionaries here. Papetoai is typical of villages on Moorea. The people live with modern materials and amenities, but the underlying culture is still intact—that is, they live in extended families, grow or catch a lot of their own food, speak Tahitian as a first language, and look to their elders for leadership. I know many of the families from having lived on Moorea since 1992, and I arrange for some of the local elders to walk us around the village and talk about

Moorea is one of the most spectacular tropical islands you'll ever find.

their lives. The local people are happy to talk with visitors who show respect for and interest in their culture." Near Papetoai there's a shallow area along the reef where local boatmen feed stingrays for visitors' pleasure. The stingrays are tame, and visitors can swim with them, even pet them. Black-tip reef sharks—very docile and interested only in morsels of tuna—will come in to be fed as well.

Your course next turns south along the west coast of Moorea. The surf is strong here as you change direction, but the large waves crashing on the reef have no impact on the lagoon, which remains calm. Soon you'll beach your craft to take in the sight of the island's largest open-air temple, or *marae*. The whole altar is made of coral, and it faces a small pass in the reef. Tour leaders take this opportunity to discuss some of the legends of Moorea and Polynesian religious beliefs. (One legend concerns the hole in the summit of Mouaputa, Moorea's most dramatic mountain peak. It's said that the hole was formed when the demigod Pai tossed his spear from Tahiti to prevent the mountain from being stolen from Hiro, the god of thieves.) Though most Mooreans have converted to Christianity, *marae* are still considered sacred places; many people believe in the presence of ancestral spirits as well as the Christian notion of God.

Your modest pension in the Haapiti area has bungalows made of bamboo and thatch. Matauvau Pass is just across the lagoon, and just beyond the pass is one of Moorea's famous surfing breaks. Some guests like to go out and watch the action; spinner dolphins also come into the pass during the day. But if you don't see spinner dolphins here, you'll certainly find them another day on the water.

The next day, you'll leave your kayak on the beach and take a leisurely hike to the Opunohu Valley. When you reach the ridge above the valley, you'll enjoy views in all directions, including back to Opunohu Bay, near where your trip began. Descending into the valley, you'll come upon many archaeological remnants—more *marae,* platforms of old houses, agricultural terraces, and archery platforms, dating back to before the arrival of the first Christian missionaries in the late 1700s. (Archery was considered a sacred sport.) Some remain as initially discovered; other have been reconstructed by archaeologists. Freshwater streams crisscross the valley, giving hikers ample opportunities to cool off with a quick dip.

A special treat awaits you after you paddle around the southern edge of Moorea and up the east side: your own South Pacific island for two nights, Motu Ahi. (*Motu* is the Polynesian term for "small island.") Accommodations are simple—open-air bungalows and a common shower facility, to keep the ecological impact on the island as low as possible. "It's like a comfortable camping experience, and the great thing is we have the islet to ourselves," Murphy says. The dawns over nearby Tahiti are brilliant, as the island is silhouetted by the sun to the east before there's an explosion of orange.

There are many recreational options on Motu Ahi. The fellow who owns the little pension has created a "lagoonarium" by fencing off a stretch of the lagoon, so it's easy to snorkel and observe colorful reef fish. There's a little break nearby if guests want to try surfing. Or you can kayak across the lagoon to the main island and hike into waterfalls with deep freshwater pools below for swimming in. "The last night on the island, we throw a big traditional feast on the beach, cooked in an *ahima'a,* or ground oven," Murphy adds. "There is usually a pig, *fafa* chicken (chicken with taro leaves), breadfruit, taro, tarua, plantains, Tahitian *po'e* (fruit-flavored manioc with coconut), and then *poisson cru* (marinated tuna). Using the *ahima'a,* all of the food (except the *poisson cru*) is essentially steamed, so it is moist but has a smoky flavor from the wood fire."

If you haven't sated your appetite for Polynesia after a week circling Moorea, Frank Murphy has the perfect coda for your visit—the add-on of a day sail to the private coral atoll of Tetiaroa, where Marlon Brando once lived. "We take a seventy-five-foot catamaran about thirty miles on the open ocean to this little island," Murphy explains. "As Moorea and Tahiti fade into the distance, you begin to see palm trees up ahead—and the reflection of a blue-green lagoon on low clouds, if there are any. When we arrive, the cat anchors, and we ride into the lagoon in a Zodiac; you have to catch the swell just right to ride over the reef. The lagoon, shallow and aquamarine, is dreamy. There's an island in the middle that hosts a colony of seabirds—brown boobies, red-footed boobies, frigate birds. If guests wish, they can paddle around in kayaks or do some snorkeling. After lunch on the beach, we'll head back out to the cat. There will be time to do a little snorkeling outside the reef. A few times, we've had the chance to swim with a humpback whale mother and calf at this spot. We sail back as the sun is beginning to sink in the sky."

11

Surf's Up at Sumba — Nihiwatu, Indonesia

WHY: Perfect your surfing with one of the world's great instructors at a
one-of-a-kind eco-lodge on a paradisiacal Indonesian island where
old ways still live.

O N ONE OF MY FIRST VISITS TO NIHIWATU, I was walking along the beach with my
board," professional surfer Terry Simms says, "when suddenly a group of water buffalo
came thundering out of the jungle. There were little naked boys—six or eight years old—herding the buffalo toward the surf. I was startled and even a little scared at first, and then I realized
that the kids had brought the buffalo to the surf so they could wash off the animals after plowing the fields. This definitely wasn't Maui!"

Former longboard champion and renowned instructor Simms was initially drawn to Nihiwatu by rumors of the proverbial perfect wave, which surf-industry insiders have dubbed "God's
Left" (as it breaks to the left). He's been drawn back again and again (with students in tow) by
the vibe of the place and by the wonderful Nihiwatu, Claude and Petra Graves's luxurious yet
sustainable resort that truly gives back to the community by plowing most profits back to islanders through a nonprofit organization.

"I believe that there are certain power points around the world that give off a positive energy," Simms says. "I've surfed all over the world, and Nihiwatu exudes some of the most powerful natural spirituality that I've experienced anywhere. Nihiwatu is actually the name for a
sacrificial rock on one edge of the beach. This beach is not just a place where the people harvest
seaweed and octopus off the reef and wash their buffalo. It's a sacred place of worship for the
local Sumbanese people, and you can feel that."

Claude and Petra Graves arrived in Sumba in 1988, after traveling throughout Indonesia,
seeking a place for a special kind of eco-resort, and the region of southwest Sumba met all their
criteria—seclusion, pristine beaches, thriving indigenous cultures where animist faiths are still
practiced, and in Nihiwatu, they found in addition a mind-blowing surf break. Their 438-acre

Terry Simms catches the perfect wave—"God's Left"—at Nihiwatu.

> "I've surfed all over the world, and Nihiwatu exudes some of the most powerful natural spirituality that I've experienced anywhere."

property wraps along a mile and a half of private beach, guarded on each end by rocky headlands that ensure privacy. Seven bungalows and three two-bedroom villas fabricated from thatch, bamboo, and wood are tucked into the trees along the ridge and house up to just twenty-five guests at a time. Each is outfitted with furniture and textiles created by Indonesian craftspeople, and balconies with comfortable rattan chairs and a daybed that offer westward vistas of the ocean and awesome sunsets. Given its romantic setting, it's not a surprise that Nihiwatu has become a favorite honeymoon retreat.

The magic of the place is apparent from the moment you arrive. "From the tiny airstrip where you land on Sumba, it's about two hours through the jungle to the entrance of Nihiwatu," Simms explains. "You come up over a hill, and there's the beach. The stunning thing is, there's no one there. No one fishing, no one walking on the beach. Most guests are pretty tired upon arrival, especially if they flew into Bali [point of departure for Sumba] the previous day. But the water is so blue and the sand so white, you get a burst of energy. If you've brought your own board, it will generally arrive at the lodge in an hour. But they have boards for guest use, and many guests will be in the water quickly."

Most world-class breaks are reliable to produce one size or type of wave, or to be at their best for a limited time. The beauty of the left break at Nihiwatu is that the waves start breaking at one foot and go all the way to twenty feet. It breaks consistently all year, the winds are complementary, and thanks to lodge rules, there are never more than nine surfers on the beach. "This is perfect for teaching," Simms says, "as there are never crowds, and there's a wide range of wave sizes to accommodate first-day surfers and experts alike. Surfing is about two things—safety and releasing your inner spirit. I try to give people a chance to experience an extreme activity without extreme risk, to have the joy and fun they may not have had since childhood.

"Standing on that beach by myself at dawn, I've experienced such a sense of unbridled joy," Simms says. "Not the satisfaction you might feel because you got a new car or your movie got made—a very pure joy simply for being there, for being alive."

The bungalows at Nihiwatu are decorated with furniture and textiles fashioned by Indonesian craftspeople.

12

ISLAND-HOPPING IN THE SEYCHELLES

WHY: Rare luxury awaits on isolated private islands in the Indian Ocean,
where special care is being taken to preserve the exotic environment.

Sun, sugary white sand, and clear, warm water. You can find them in the Caribbean. But in the Seychelles, 1,000 miles off the coast of Tanzania, you'll not simply enjoy beach retreat bliss; you'll revel in exotic flora and fauna, plus the aura of exclusivity and solitude that the region's many private islands can provide. Little known ten years ago, the Seychelles saw their profile soar after celebrities such as Pierce Brosnan and Paul McCartney began vacationing there.

"I first went to the Seychelles in 1999 and returned again a few years ago," Laura Begley, deputy editor of *Travel + Leisure,* says. "The islands have undergone an incredible transformation in the last decade. They've always been beautiful and exotic, but now they also boast an excellent assortment of first-rate resorts. During my visits, I had the sense that local people were thrilled to have tourists coming, and not just for the economic benefit. I think they feel a bit stranded, being so geographically isolated. They seemed genuinely happy to have a chance to share their islands with the world—to have the world, in a manner of speaking, come to them. This was reflected in their fine attention to service."

The 115 islands that comprise the Seychelles present as idyllic a tropical environment as one could imagine. Given the number of islands and the unique appeal of their respective resorts, one of the challenges would-be Seychelles visitors face is deciding which island to visit. One option is to hedge your bets and visit a different island for each night of your stay, hopping from one to the next by speedboat, helicopter, or prop plane, as Begley did.

Your Seychelles island-hopping tour will likely begin on the main island of Mahé (the administrative center of the Seychelles, where the international airport is situated), at the Banyan Tree Seychelles resort. The resort is set on Intendance Bay, on a half-mile stretch of talcum-powder beach. Each of the sixty villas—some beachside, some on the hillside overlooking the Indian Ocean—has a private pool. Like other Banyan Tree properties, this one offers a top-flight selection of spa services—including spiced honey wraps and tamarind-and-oatmeal body polishes. Begley experienced the Tropical Rainmist, a three-hour treatment that combines a body scrub

Each of the ten villas at North Island has a plunge pool and sala *(gazebo) on a deck that overlooks the Indian Ocean.*

(scented salt or orange and yogurt), a moisturizer of honey and milk, a steam bath, and a massage. "The Tropical Rainmist made me feel like I was getting a treatment in the jungle itself," Begley says. "The connection to the tropical surroundings made it special." Perhaps the best part of any treatment at Banyan Tree is the spa itself. There are eight treatment rooms, hidden amid jungle and granite boulders. Some of the rooms have views looking out across the Indian Ocean. "You can have the doors open to the fresh air and tropical breezes, which I preferred," Begley adds, "with the sound of the birds right outside."

The isle of Praslin and Lémuria Resort were next on Begley's itinerary. In addition to the requisite pristine beach (actually, three) and full-service spa, Lémuria also boasts the Seychelles' only eighteen-hole golf course. The resort's suites and villas—built on the edge of the rain forest using wood, marble, and pink granite—all look out on the ocean. "Lémuria takes special pains to keep the lighting low so it doesn't disturb sea turtles that lay eggs on the beach at night," Begley says—a challenge somewhat germane to the Seychelles! One of Praslin's treasures is the Vallée de Mai, a pristine palm forest in a valley near the center of the island, once thought to be the site of the biblical Garden of Eden. Vallée de Mai is home to the coco-de-mer palm, producer of the world's largest seed, which can reach weights of nearly 50 pounds. It also provides

The Vallée de Mai was once thought to be the site of the biblical Garden of Eden.

habitat for a number of rare birds, including a subspecies of black parrot that's found only on Praslin.

At Cousine Island, it's not sea turtles that guests must contend with but the nineteen Aldabra giant tortoises that call this private island home. These land-based reptiles, which take their name from the island of Aldabra, near the bottom of the Seychelles archipelago, can regularly grow to 500 pounds. Their continued presence is part of the conservation effort launched by the island's owner, Malcolm Keeley, a billionaire granite magnate who rents the island's four guest villas to support his environmental mission. "There are sixteen staff members to attend to a maximum of ten guests, and day-trippers are not allowed," Begley explains. "While Cousine is not a high-style getaway, there was nothing like waking up in the morning and seeing tortoises outside my front door, or walking down a path and seeing a magpie robin, one of fewer than two hundred on earth." Each of the four guest villas includes a whirlpool bath and offers ocean views. Meals are taken in an open-air dining area in the Pavillion, which also houses a lounge and library, adjacent to a freshwater pool. The rest of Cousine is given over to plants and animals that have been gradually reintroduced to the island as part of Keeley's effort to return it to its pre–French colonial condition.

The high point of Begley's island-hopping excursion was reached at North Island, another guest-only getaway, overseen by Wilderness Safaris. The overall design concept here is barefoot luxury; one of North Island's architects, Silvio Rech, dubbed the resort's look "couture Robinson Crusoe." Each of the ten thatched-roof villas is nearly 5,000 square feet and has two bedrooms, allowing a couple or small family ample space to spread out. In a nod to the resort's eco-sensitive charter to reinstate indigenous flora and fauna, nonnative trees have been taken down; their lumber has been used in villa construction, and their bleached limbs decorate stairways and balustrades. The master bathroom has a marble tub and two showers, one inside and one out. The turquoise Indian Ocean is ever in view from each villa's expansive deck, where guests will enjoy a private plunge pool and a linen-cloaked *sala* (African gazebo). Each of the villas has a kitchen, though most guests will opt to dine at the Piazza, a social center that includes North Island's library, outdoor-activities center, lounge, and freshwater pool; the overall schema is similar to that on Cousine Island, though on a grander scale. Chef David Godin interviews guests about their dining preferences and develops daily menus to delight individual palates, using local seafood and Creole seasonings whenever tastes permit. In addition to the ten "standard" villas, there's the North Island Villa, which includes a private outdoor spa area.

It's impossible to stare out at the crystalline sea without yearning to get in it—or least on it. North Island can outfit deep-sea fishers in search of yellowfin tuna, fly fishers hoping to hook bonefish on the island's flats, and kayakers and snorkelers happy to skim along the surface and take in the sights. The Seychelles are considered one of the world's great scuba destinations, with underwater visibility up to 150 feet, and North Island has a complete dive shop with certified instructors. Animals commonly seen include trumpetfish, batfish, paper fish, raggy scorpion fish, stonefish, emperor angelfish, great barracuda, rock mover wrasse, huge shoals of fusilier, white-tip reef shark, and hawksbill and green turtle. Divers may have a chance to swim with the world's largest fish, whale sharks, which frequent these waters.

IN THE JUNGLE

THE WORLD'S GREAT JUNGLES HOLD A FASCINATION FOR INTREPID TRAVELERS. PART OF THE ALLURE IS THE JUNGLES' VERY IMPENE-trability, which shields these environs from outside eyes, heightening their mystery. Another draw is the plentitude of plant and animal life that tropical rain forests nurture—charismatic species like tigers and birds of paradise, and countless plants, insects, and reptiles that have not yet been classified by scientists. In places like Amazonia, Borneo, and Papua New Guinea, there's an exhilaration that comes with the realization that many of the rain forest's secrets have yet to be revealed.

It used to be that a trip into jungle terrain required braving the elements in a bare-bones manner, with a small tent—or perhaps just a bedroll and a machete. While some prefer to travel light (and a few such trips are highlighted here), jungle visitors need not forgo amenities; indeed, guests at Abu Camp ("Elephant Safari in Botswana") or on the *Road to Mandalay* ("Into the Heart of Myanmar") will find surroundings and service every bit as sumptuous as at their favorite hotel.

Ambua Lodge rests on the slopes overlooking Tari Valley in Papua New Guinea, where thirteen species of birds of paradise await.

13

Elephant Safari in Botswana

WHY: Explore the remote Okavango Delta by elephant, and luxuriate in accommodations that set a new standard for safari elegance.

Spying a herd of elephants is undoubtedly a high point for anyone who's taken an African safari. Abu Camp in Botswana puts a different twist on the safari experience, as you conduct your animal watching atop the back of an elephant. Abu Camp sits in a 400,000-acre private reserve in the Okavango Delta, the world's largest inland delta. The wetland sanctuary that flourishes here—an immense series of lagoons, channels, and palm-filled islands—supports a wide assortment of plains game, including zebras, impalas, tsessebes (a species of antelope), wildebeests, buffalos, warthog, leopards, cheetahs, lions, and herds of wild elephants. Five hundred bird species also call the Okavango home.

Next, there's the camp itself, a portrait of luxury made all the more astounding given its remote surroundings. Abu Camp consists of six canvas tents elevated on wooden decks, with a viewing station overlooking the nearby lagoon. Each tent has polished wood floors, mahogany sleigh-style beds, and spacious en suite bathrooms with large copper bathtubs. The lounge/dining area is appointed with large sofas and portraits of the camp's main residents, the elephants; there's even a small library that boasts an extensive collection of elephant-oriented research material.

"The food and service are impeccable," Amanda Hyde, commissioning editor of *The Sunday Times Travel Magazine* (London), says. "There's a maximum of twelve guests at a time, and from a glance in the guest book, you see that they are quite used to hosting the rich and famous. The husband and wife who run the lodge are traditional Brits, and they create a convivial environment where visitors feel more like friends than lodge guests.

The main attraction at Abu is its trained elephants and the chance to take in the Okavango from a perch on their backs. At the time of this writing, there are nine animals in the camp's herd. When guests arrive at Abu Camp they are introduced to each elephant and briefed on the

Guests, elephants, and their mahouts set out on a dawn game-viewing safari.

animal's background. "Each of the elephants has not only its own name but its own personality," Hyde explains. "Some are playful, some are naughty, a few are not so used to carrying people on their backs." At night, camp hosts give informal talks on the animals and the Okavango. But your real introduction comes the next morning, when you climb upon Cathy, the lead elephant, or one of her associates.

Each elephant has a handler—a mahout—who rides on the elephant's neck, with his legs behind the animal's ears, and who has a warm, trusting relationship with his animal. Behind the mahout is a saddle of sorts, and that's where you sit; the elephant is squatting when you climb on, and you hold on tight when it gets to its feet. (If you have an aversion to taking your pachyderm mount, you can walk alongside the elephant.) Each morning you take a different route through the wetlands. Riding on the elephants, you're able to get much closer to the wildlife than you would in a Range Rover; the animals see elephants, not people, so they're not put off.

"We didn't see any of the big cats on our walks, but we did come upon kudus, zebras, and hippos," Hyde says. "It didn't matter much whether we saw lots of wildlife; being on an elephant in this wild setting, watching the members of the herd interact with each other, was enough. When you're out on a walk, the little elephants trek along. If they can't find their mom, they make funny noises and wiggle their ears around. On one hike, a young elephant named Little Abu found a snake. This seemed to traumatize him, but he was soon led away by the mahout like a naughty schoolboy.

"My favorite part of the safari was seeing the relationship between the mahouts and the elephants. They're so kind and caring. The mahouts play with the young elephants as if they are children or puppies."

The lodge at Abu Camp is elegantly appointed and boasts a library of elephant-related works.

14

RAFTING THE MOSQUITO COAST, HONDURAS

WHY: Rafting the Rió Plátano through North America's largest
virgin rain forest, you'll explore isolated archaeological sites,
see rare animals, and experience true wilderness.

*T*HE *MOSQUITO COAST* IS THE TITLE OF A FINE NOVEL by Paul Theroux involving an alienated Massachusetts man who moves his family to a Central American rain forest to live a simpler life. (The "Mosquito" of Mosquito Coast refers to one of the region's indigenous peoples, the Miskito, not to the insect.) Things did not go well for the fictional family, who lacked the expertise to adapt to their sometimes-hostile surroundings. With the crack team that the Mesoamerican Ecotourism Alliance has assembled—including archaeologist Chris Begley, naturalist Robert Gallardo, and lead guide Jorge Salaveri—you'll have on hand the expertise to safely experience this wild country in eastern Honduras and to gain a better understanding of its flora, fauna, and people. This is a true wilderness adventure; traveling mostly by inflatable raft, you'll have no contact with the outside world.

"Some people think of La Mosquitia as a miniature Amazon," Chris Begley explains. He has explored the jungles of Central America for fifteen years and has been involved in scientific expeditions on the remote Mosquito Coast. "One reason for this comparison is that the Río Plátano Biosphere Reserve is the largest piece of intact rain-forest habitat [2 million acres] outside of the Amazon. Another reason is the sense of scale that you get here. The Amazon is so big, it's in some ways hard to feel a connection. You feel like an observer, rather than a part of it. On the Mosquito Coast, the hilly terrain makes the scope more contained. The river is small enough so you feel like part of it as you make your way to the sea."

Your journey into the jungles of Mosquitia begins on foot with an 11-mile hike over two days from the frontier village of Bonanza into the interior. There are no roads into the Río Plátano; hiking in is the only option. Your gear is carried in on pack mules (and later strapped to the rafts), and each night your guides will set up a basic, comfortable camp. (There's one guide for each three visitors, four for an expedition of twelve guests.) It's hot in the Río Plátano Biosphere, and your tents have four windows for superior ventilation, and thick Therm-a-Rest

Guests run Class III rapids on the Río Plátano.

sleeping pads. Tarps are set up to provide shelter from periodic rain, and meals are taken under the tarps, with the rafts doubling as your seating. The river is your bathtub, and biodegradable soap is provided.

The following day, you push along on foot to the raft put-in, pausing along the way to marvel at the petroglyphs and stone monuments at Lancetillal. "We've learned that the people who lived here between A.D. 500 and 1200 combined many cultural traits common to people to the south, such as unpainted pottery and tripod grinding stones, with traits of the Mesoamerican cultures such as the Maya to the north," Begley says. "This is a real crossroads, with Mesoamerican ball courts found at the same site as with all the unpainted, monochrome pottery and the tripod grinding stones. No other groups share traits in this way."

The next day the rafts are pumped up and loaded and you'll get a safety briefing on river dos and don'ts—and then you're off into the heart of this vast wilderness. The rafts, between 11 and 13 feet in length, are constructed of ultra-durable Hypalon and accommodate three guests and a guide. "Walking through the jungle for a few days before getting on the rafts makes the river portion of the trip that much more exciting," Begley says. "By the time you've reached the river, you have some familiarity and appreciation of the terrain. You've worked somewhat hard to get here, and now, for the next week, you can sit back and enjoy it."

One of the reasons you float on the Río Plátano is to catch glimpses of the many animals that call the jungle home. "When we're walking through the jungle, the animals hear us from a mile away and make themselves scarce," Begley explains. "When we're floating down on the raft, our approach is almost silent, and we come up very close upon the animals, which are drawn to the river to drink." White-faced capuchin and spider monkeys are commonly seen, as well as white-lipped peccaries (a species of wild pig), anteaters, sloths, river otters, and five species of toucans. Baird's tapirs are frequently encountered as well; these creatures, which are shaped like large pigs and most notable for their short, prehensile snouts, are related to horses and rhinoceroses. "On one trip, the raft in front of mine floated up on a puma," Begley recalls. "The puma and jaguar are here, as are harpy eagles, but they're seldom seen. Unless there's been hard rain, the water is crystal clear, and there's a great deal of aquatic life, including giant freshwater prawns that almost resemble lobsters."

This is a true wilderness adventure; traveling mostly by inflatable raft, you'll have no contact with the outside world.

On a river trip like this, you soon settle into a pace—a pace that the river dictates. After a leisurely hot breakfast of oatmeal or pancakes, your guides break camp and you load the rafts to continue down the river. Scanning the thick canopy of foliage that envelops the river, you may spy a chestnut-mandible toucan or scarlet macaw—or dwell on the thought that there are no human settlements for many miles in any direction—and no other people. Blue morpho butterflies offer a vibrant, fluttering display of color against the greenery. While not a white-knuckle white-water river, the Río Plátano has enough rapids to keep your blood pumping—particularly el Subterraneo, a mile-long gorge of Class III rapids that requires a brief portage. "You have to work a bit to get the raft through places, and it can get your adrenaline going," Begley explains, "but our guides know the river well. There are times when you're going down a set of rapids and a spectacular animal appears. You're trying to watch the animal, negotiate the rapids, and take in the rain forest at the same time. It's such a rich, multi-layered experience."

There's nothing like a river trip to build a hearty appetite, and wayfarers on the Río Plátano are well fed. "Dinners are the big meal," Begley says, "and Jorge is an excellent camp cook. He makes soups, pastas, and a local dish called *baleadas,* a combination of flour tortillas, beans, and cheese. We often supplement our meals with fresh fish caught from the river."

Travelers continue to come upon archaeological sites for much of the float. One of the most enigmatic for Chris Begley is an abandoned village that's come to be called Los Metates. The site has several large grinding stones. Some may have been used for corn, but others, which have elaborate markings, likely had some symbolic purpose. "What's very curious is that in addition to the large stones, there are literally thousands of miniature ones, the *metates,*" Begley explains. "These stones fit in your hand. They seem like small effigies of the larger stones, and no one knows their purpose—were they an offering of sorts, or a tax that was paid?"

Near the bottom of the river, you begin to pass settlements of Garifuna, Pech, and Miskito peoples. "Our guides hail from some of these villages, and we're often invited to visit their houses, and a community party breaks out," Begley says. "Thanks to the low level of tourism here, there are no stilted 'watch the indigenous folks dance' programs. We're part of the extended family. If villagers bring out their drums and start playing and dancing, we join in. There's nothing artificial about it. Often our group will leave, and the party will still be going on."

15

WILD BORNEO

WHY: This tour de force lets you experience some of the world's great jungle
and marine habitats and their rare inhabitants—including wild orangutans.

STRADDLING THE EQUATOR NEAR THE CENTER OF INDONESIA, Borneo is the
world's third-largest island, roughly the size of Texas. Thanks in part to its sultry climate—
Charles Darwin once called the island "one great wild untidy luxuriant hothouse"—Borneo
boasts an incomparable level of biodiversity. It's home to more than 15,000 *known* plants, 350
bird species, 220 mammals, and 150 reptiles and amphibians. The waters off of Sabah support
3,000 fish and hundreds of coral species. Biologists believe that there could be thousands of
additional plant and animal species that have yet to be identified on the island. According to a
study published by the World Wildlife Fund, 361 new flora and fauna have been discovered just
since 1996.

"On much of the island, the rain forest that orangutans and other rare animals call home is
being chopped down and otherwise exploited at an alarming rate," says Asia travel consultant
Tom Lastick. "In Sabah, the Malaysian government is doing a better job of preserving the land.
But even here, you can't promise that the next generation will be able to see orangutans in the
wild."

To begin your trip you'll fly into Kota Kinabalu, the gateway to Sabah and the province's capital. You'll spend the first two nights of your stay at the Shangri-La's Tanjung Aru Resort and Spa
on a peninsula in the South China Sea. Your foray into the field begins as you fly to Sabah's eastern
coast and board a speedboat to Selingan Island. One of three islands that make up Turtle Islands
National Park, Selingan is a nesting ground for endangered green and hawksbill turtles. You'll do
some snorkeling in the afternoon to explore the local reefs, and in the evening, rangers take you
to watch the green turtles come ashore to lay their eggs.

The next morning you'll return to the mainland and visit the Sepilok Orangutan Rehabilitation Center, where you'll have your first opportunity to encounter orangutans. Sepilok is one of
a number of rehabilitation centers in Borneo where orphaned animals are taken. Young orang-

The lowland rain forest of the Danum Valley is considered to be the oldest forest in the world.

utans don't have skills to survive in the wild. They rely on their mothers until the age of four and often live with them for several years after. The animals at Sepilok are not in the wild per se, but the reserve is a natural environment where they are free to move about.

There's a chance that you'll see orangutans as you walk the trails that wind through the preserve, but you're certain to see them when they're called in at feeding time. "The rangers bring the apes in from the surrounding forests with a *whoop, whoop* kind of call," Lastick explains. "You soon can hear rustling from afar. It gets louder as the apes get closer, and soon you can see movement in the trees. Then the orangutans come swinging through, from branch to

Biologists believe that there could be thousands of additional plant and animal species that have yet to be identified on Borneo.

branch, at great speed—it's a heart-pounding moment. Watching these animals up close, you can't help but be touched by their inquisitiveness. When you look one in the eye, you feel like they're checking you out as well."

From Sepilok, a small boat takes you up the Kinabatangan River into the dense rain forest of Kinabatangan Wildlife Sanctuary, which provides protected habitat for Malaysia's highest concentration of orangutans. The Sukau Rainforest Lodge—one of Borneo's award-winning ecolodges—will be your home within the sanctuary for the next few nights. Built in traditional longhouse style, Sukau is comfortable if not elaborate; rooms have twin beds with attached bathrooms and showers, and you can enjoy a cold beer or lemonade on the lodge's open deck overlooking the river. Alfresco dinner by candlelight is available at the lodge's restaurant, Melapo. (Cuisine in Borneo is a mélange of flavors, a mix of Chinese, Thai, Malaysian, and European traditions.)

From Sukau, you'll take locally handcrafted wooden boats upriver to explore the jungle and the oxbow lakes that have formed adjacent to some of the river's larger bends; electric-powered outboards allow for silent approaches. Orangutans are very spread out, as each adult needs a great deal of terrain to find enough food to survive. Still, it's not uncommon to come upon orangutans up in the trees, though you'll only catch a glimpse; the apes are shy in the wild and will be gone in a flash when they sense your presence. Kinabatangan is also home to endangered proboscis monkeys, long-tailed macaques, leaf monkeys, gibbons, Asian elephants, Sumatran rhinos, reticulated pythons, monitor lizards, and hundreds of bird species.

You'll next be transported by motorcoach to Danum Valley, in a region called the Heart of

Borneo. This is Malaysia's largest remaining tract of virgin lowland rain forest and is believed to be the oldest forest in the world, dating back 100 million years. You'll use the Borneo Rainforest Lodge as a base for the next three nights to continue your pursuit of orangutans and the area's other mammal life. Rooms are in chalets that rest on stilts above the jungle floor and include private bathrooms (with shower) and a balcony. The lodge itself overlooks the river and houses a lounge with full bar and the dining room.

Danum Valley is a celebrated birding locale, boasting some 275 species. You'll have a chance to sight them from the lodge's many trails and its 150-foot-tall canopy walkway, which allows you to look *down* on the avian life. Birds found here include all eight species of hornbill, Bornean bristlehead, Bornean ground cuckoo, great argus pheasant, and white-fronted falconet; the lodge's resident naturalists are on hand to help experienced and new birders locate the region's signature species. "The rhinoceros hornbill is a wonderful bird that you're very likely to see," Lastick says. "You can hear it whooshing from what seems like a mile away, and then it passes over you with its tremendous wingspan." Early risers will often wake to the sound of gibbons calling; to take advantage of the best wildlife viewing in both Danum and Kinabatangan, you'll want to be up at first light and use the sultry midday to catch up on your sleep.

Next your exploration of Borneo will return to marine environs. A speedboat races you to the island of Mabul and Borneo Divers Mabul Resort, considered a must-visit spot among scuba aficionados. Guests stay in chalets constructed from local hardwoods, with bath and a private verandah; the dining complex doubles as your socializing center (karaoke is available some nights). Here you'll have two days to snorkel among some of the Indo-Pacific's richest marine biodiversity. Sipadan island, just a short boat ride away from Mabul, offers dramatically different waters. "Mabul has gently sloping reefs," Lastick says, "and the waters are fairly shallow, which makes for easy snorkeling. We see lots of what scuba divers like to call 'critters'—small but extremely interesting animals like harlequin shrimp, cuttlefish, and boxer crabs. At Sipadan, the water drops off abruptly to depths of over two thousand feet. Here the draw is the many big sea animals that are drawn toward the surface by the upwelling of ocean currents." You might swim with turtles, manta rays, barracudas, and whale sharks.

16

INTO THE HEART OF MYANMAR

WHY: A cruise up the Irrawaddy River on the *Road to Mandalay* luxury vessel
exposes you to the sights and culture of Myanmar as this isolated nation
slowly opens it doors to the world.

T HE IRRAWADDY RUNS OVER 1,300 MILES, NEARLY THE entire length of Myanmar
(formerly known as Burma), which borders China to the north, Laos and Thailand to the
east, and India and Bangladesh to the west. Before railroads and automobiles, it was nicknamed
the Road to Mandalay, hence the name of the ship. The *Road to Mandalay* sails through much of
the year from the city of Mandalay south to Pagan. Myanmar travel pioneer Thomas Evers-
Swindell's favorite time to sail is the summer, when the river is high enough for the boat to make
passage to Bhamo in the north. As regional director for Asia for Orient-Express Hotels, he says,
"This part of Myanmar is still virtually inaccessible by road," he explains, "and as you go upriver,
and head into the much less visited parts of the country, every day is a new experience." The
population becomes more dispersed and the villages more removed from modernity. You leave
behind the dry zone of Myanmar—marked by sparse vegetation and arid hills—and pass through
countryside that's considerably more lush. In the final days traveling north, the river narrows
into two very distinct defiles (gorges) and the terrain is markedly steeper.

The Myanmar sun can be strong and the air is humid, but the *Road to Mandalay* provides a
comfortable place of repose. The ship started its life in 1964 in Germany, cruising the Rhine,
but was acquired by Orient-Express (a luxury travel company that also operates the famed
Orient-Express trains) and refurbished in 1994. When it arrived in Mandalay, it was given a Burmese makeover, including locally woven cane furniture for many of the public areas. All staterooms are air-conditioned and furnished with fine linens and Burmese-style fabrics. For the
Bhamo adventure, the boat accommodates a maximum of eighty passengers in fifty-two staterooms. Meals are served in the *Road to Mandalay*'s restaurant at your leisure, and run the gamut
from classic French to modern Burmese; lunch tends toward Asian dishes like tempura, curry,

The U Min Kyaukse pagoda is one of many fantastical devotional edifices along the Irrawaddy.

and coconut rice, while dinner may include crayfish with white wine and pomelo sauce and parmesan crisps or seared duck breast with potato galette and ginger butter sauce.

By Western standards, the villages on the upper sections of the Irrawaddy are primitive, with houses made of wood and local *attap* palm-style woven walls and roofs. There's usually no electricity, running water, or sewage systems. Meals are cooked on wood fires. Most houses are raised on stilts; this allows for better ventilation and also for the variation in river levels during the monsoon season. Animals are kept on the ground, and people live above. The arrival of the *Road to Mandalay* is a major event for villagers, and they respond enthusiastically.

Myanmar was under British rule from 1885 until 1948, and several of the bigger towns on the upper river—such as Katha and Bhamo—have a distinctive colonial feel. In Katha, the English Club (where much of the action of George Orwell's novel *Burmese Days* takes place) is still largely intact. Katha has a bustling local market, which you'll have a chance to tour by trishaw (Burmese parlance for the bike taxis known as rickshaws); on the boat's return through Katha, you can take an antique train into the thick Kachin jungle to a remote forest station and get a taste of the rugged, almost impenetrable terrain that extends beyond the Irrawaddy's high-water mark.

As the *Road to Mandalay* moves upriver, the jungle seems to envelop the ship. The thick rain forest sweeps down to the shore, mountains appear in the distance, and mist rises off the river. At each of the two defiles you pass through, the river narrows and sheer cliffs drop right down to the water. Eventually the ship slowly retraces its path downriver, giving guests a chance to appreciate the jungle scenery from a different perspective. You might catch a glimpse of the endangered Irrawaddy dolphin, which can exist in fresh and salt water.

On your trip south, you'll continue beyond the city of Mandalay to Pagan, a former center of Buddhist spirituality comparable in scope and grandeur to Cambodia's Angkor Wat. Between the eleventh and thirteenth centuries, countless pagodas and temples were built along the Irrawaddy; historians believe there were as many as thirteen thousand religious structures in Pagan before Kublai Khan's forces swept through in A.D. 1287. Today, more than two thousand structures still stand. The temples of Dhammayangyi and Shwezigon are especially striking for their grand scale and opulence. Watching the first rays of sun reflect off the temples from the river is a sublime experience and a fitting conclusion to your exploration of this remote nation.

During the summer rainy season the Road to Mandalay *plies the upper reaches of the Irrawaddy.*

17

ON THE TRAIL OF THE TIGER IN NEPAL

WHY: Tracking wild Bengal tigers in the subtropical forest of the Royal Chitwan
National Park of Nepal is best from an elephant-back perspective.

WHILE THE NUMBER OF BENGAL TIGERS IS DWINDLING worldwide, populations in Royal Chitwan National Park in south-central Nepal are stable. Visitors here
have an excellent chance to see one of these graceful and powerful predators up close in the
wild, on an elephant-back excursion with Tiger Tops Jungle Lodge.

Most visitors come to Chitwan after a few days in the Nepalese capital of Kathmandu, and the
contrast between the frenetic city at the base of the Himalayas and this pastoral lowland is great.
On the ride from the airport in the town of Meghauli to where you'll cross the Gandak River
(also called the Narayani) to reach the national park (roughly an hour's drive), you'll pass through
several villages that are home to the Tharu people, an ethnic group that has lived here for millennia. Over generations, the Tharu have cleared much of the forest adjacent to the national park to
cultivate rice, and in the fall, the main growing season, you'll pass paddies cloaked in neon green.
When you reach the Gandak, a staff member from Tiger Tops Jungle Lodge is waiting with a
wooden canoe to spirit you across. As he poles the canoe, be on the lookout for one of the park's
residents, the gharial crocodile which can grow to 20 feet in length; you'll generally first see their
eyes and nostrils as they hover just below the surface. Tharu fishermen may be on the river too,
casting their nets, perhaps with their family in tow.

In contrast to the land outside the park, Chitwan has intact ecosystems, with flora endemic
to the region—stately sal trees, a hardwood species, and native grasses, which grow to over
20 feet in height and provide excellent cover for the park's many mammal species.

Tiger Tops is the longest-standing lodge operation in Chitwan (indeed, in Nepal) and offers
several accommodation options. The Jungle Lodge houses guests in rooms fashioned from local
woods and thatch; they rest on stilts and are fondly referred to as the tree houses. Rooms
are appointed with Nepalese textiles and en suite bathrooms. Guests at the lodge take meals

*Tigers are the primary viewing quarry for visitors to Tiger Tops Jungle Lodge, but other rare animals—including the Asian one-
horned rhinoceros—are also encountered.*

and socialize in a *gol ghar*, a circular dining room/bar (based on a typical Tharu design) with an open hearth. The lodge has its own organic farm just outside the park, which supplies many of the vegetables—bitter gourd (which tastes much better than it sounds), potatoes, radishes, spinach, and onions—which are featured in Tiger Top's curries and lentil dishes. Nepal produces an intoxicating array of spices, and locally sourced garlic, ginger, cumin, coriander, turmeric, nutmeg, black pepper, saffron, chiles, and cilantro all find their way into meals; chile-lime chutney is a favored condiment.

A few miles from the Jungle Lodge on the banks of the Reu River is the Tiger Tops Tented Camp, with twelve safari-style tents (with attached bathrooms), a *gol ghar* for cocktails, and a dining tent. From a raised platform outside the *gol ghar*, you can often spy game grazing on the grasslands below—including the Asian one-horned rhinoceros, an animal unique to Nepal and India—with a cold drink in hand. "There's a strong Gurkha influence at Tiger Tops, and as a result, drinks that include Khukri rum, are a mainstay," explains luxury travel consultant Sasha Lehman. The Gurkhas are a brigade of Nepalese soldiers that have fought for Great Britain since the early 1800s, and the Brits introduced these soldiers to rum; Khukri rum comes in a bottle shaped like the Gurkhas' traditional weapon, a curved sword of the same name.

Tiger tracking is a morning affair, and after a light breakfast of freshly made biscuits and tea, you'll join your fellow trackers and meet your ride elephants—generally five or six—and their mahouts (elephant handlers). Trackers will have already been out in the park to search for signs of tigers—paw prints, bedding spots, or paths through the grass. Their advance work will help focus the group's tracking efforts. Guests ride on a seat strapped across the elephant's back, and the mahout rests upon its neck. There's always a lead elephant, which not only walks in front but keeps track of the others; if an elephant straggles behind, the lead animal will groan and grunt until the laggard catches up. When the elephants pick up the scent of a tiger (usually after the naturalist or mahout has spotted signs), they will sometimes begin to run and/or trumpet; excitement escalates as they grunt more frequently and flap their ears to communicate with one another. If they come upon a tiger, they will position themselves around the animal in a semicircle, as if pursuing a defense strategy.

"I'll never forget a leisurely morning when I was out on a game walk," Lehman says. "We weren't seeing much wildlife, but I was enjoying the rhythm of the elephant's steps when all of a sudden, without warning, my lumbering giant became a galloping force. There in my sight line were the head of my elephant and a flash of orange set against the brilliant green grass. The moment was gone in a second, but it was exhilarating to have such proximity to the king and queen of the jungle."

18

Birding in Papua New Guinea

WHY: There's no better place to see fantastical birds of paradise—and the aboriginal people whose traditions are interwoven with the birds' plumage— than Papua New Guinea's Tari Valley.

MANY BIRDWATCHERS CONSIDER BIRDS OF PARADISE TO BE the most exotic, fantastic birds on earth. And most birding experts agree that there's no better place to observe the bird of paradise species than the Tari Valley, in the Southern Highlands region of Papua New Guinea.

The preferred base of operations for birders and other naturalists visiting the Tari Valley is Ambua Lodge. Ambua rests high on the slopes of Tari Valley and can be reached only by small plane from Mount Hagen. The thrill of a trip here begins with the flight in; the plane wings over the peaks of Mount Giluwe and high-altitude grasslands before descending to the lodge's private airstrip, high on the slopes of Tari Valley, a riot of lush forest greens punctuated by the bright hues of orchids and rhododendrons. "The airstrip runs uphill, which gives you an odd sensation," says Jonathan Rossouw, a birding expert with more than twenty-five years' experience in the field. "All around you there's thick forest. You eventually notice Ambua Lodge nestled in a little clearing. There's immediately the sense that you've come to a very special place. This sense is accentuated when you come upon the spectacular ribbon-tailed astrapia right in the gardens of the lodge."

Thanks to its 7,000-foot elevation, Ambua spares its guests the intense heat that is not uncommon in Papua New Guinea's lower valleys. Since its inception in 1990, the lodge has been celebrated for both its ecologically responsible design and its understated luxury. From your perch at Ambua, you can peer out over a valley that's changed little in thousands of years. The smoke of the cooking fires of valley tribal people mixes with passing clouds; at times, the pounding of kundu drums can be heard.

Reference books will tell you that New Guinea is the second-largest island in the world, and

FOLLOWING PAGES *Ambua Lodge offers jaw-dropping views over Tari Valley.*

thanks to its size, cultural diversity, and biodiversity, many think of New Guinea as a continent unto itself. Papua New Guinea (which comprises the eastern half of the landmass) has an area slightly larger than California and more than 850 indigenous languages, with most of its citizens living close to the land. Its varied landscape, ranging from lowland tropical rain forests to highland cloud forests, is home to 5 to 10 percent of the total species on the planet, many of which are found nowhere else. These include many species of birds of paradise.

"As a group, there's nothing that equals birds of paradise in my mind," Rossouw enthuses. "They're so diverse in plumage, so diverse in their breeding displays." Their habitat ranges from elevations of almost 10,000 feet to the jungle floor; their size ranges from 6 inches to 44 inches long. One characteristic shared almost universally across the species is the splendid plumage of the males. Once the feathers of birds of paradise were discovered by the outside world, a thriving trade in the plumes evolved. Legal trade in skins and feathers was banned in Europe and the United States in the early twentieth century.

Accompanied by local guides, you'll set out on narrow but well-marked trails through a forest of elfin trees encrusted in moss and lichen. "Around Tari Valley, you'll see both species that you'd find in the higher altitudes, like King of Saxony birds of paradise and brown sicklebill, and lower-altitude species like blue birds of paradise and Stephanie's astrapia," Rossouw says. "These are wild creatures, and there's never a guarantee that you'll see all of them, but the guides are excellent and know where the birds are most likely found. I'll never forget the sight of a King of Saxony bird of paradise on its display perch near Tari Gap, above Ambua Lodge. This bird has incredibly long plumes that come from the back of its head. When it's displaying [trying to attract a mate], the male bobs back and forth, then suddenly leans forward, dropping its plumes over its head and moving them vigorously from side to side. It's an almost unbelievable sight; if it doesn't move you to become a passionate birder, nothing will."

One fascinating aspect of a trip to Ambua is the opportunity to visit the Huli Wigmen, a tribe of New Guineans that have lived in the Tari Valley for thousands of years. The lives of the Huli people and local avian species are uniquely interwoven. "The Wigmen create the most ornate headdresses you can imagine, using their own hair and feathers from Stephanie's astrapia, raggiana, and blue birds of paradise," Rossouw explains. It takes years for the men to grow their hair long enough to cut so they can create wigs. Guests from Ambua are welcome to visit the small Huli settlements at the bottom of the valley and may be treated to a performance of the bird dance, where the Wigmen hop and call in mimicry of the birds of paradise that they venerate.

The Raggiana bird of paradise, one of thirteen bird of paradise species you're likely to encounter in Tari Valley.

19

ROUGHING IT ON THE AMAZON IN PERU

WHY: An exploration of the Upper Amazon with guide Bill Lamar puts you in dug-out canoes and has you camping in tarps on the forest floor to get an explorer's sense of the South American jungle.

THE UPPER AMAZON RIVER, WITH ITS SEEMINGLY IMPENETRABLE jungles, voracious piranhas, and rumors of gold, has captured westerners' imagination for centuries. Spanish explorers first ventured upriver in the sixteenth century; Portuguese adventurers followed one hundred years later. Theodore Roosevelt traveled here shortly after his defeat in the presidential election of 1912, seeking therapy for mind and body. He very nearly expired from malaria and a leg infection, due to poor planning by Mariano da Silva Rondon, his guide and a noted Amazonian explorer of the day.

When Delta's *Sky* magazine editor David Bailey and his longtime canoeing buddy Bob Bird embarked on a lifelong dream of exploring the off-the-beaten path Upper Amazon in Peru, they understood the importance of finding the right leader. That someone was Bill Lamar. He's been running tours up and down the Amazon since the early nineties and is an adjunct professor of biology at the University of Texas at Arlington and the University of Kansas, and associate herpetologist at the National Serpentarium in San José, Costa Rica. "From the start, Lamar warned us that we'd be spending the next two weeks on more of an un-trip than a trip," Bailey says. " 'The region is so vast,' Lamar said, 'all you can do in two weeks is sort of flit around like a hummingbird. In the rain forest, the only way to garner a measure of control is by first jettisoning any attempt to gain or maintain control. The Amazon foils all plans and takes everything.' "

The Amazon stretches some 4,000 miles; adding in its tributaries, the Amazon system encompasses 50,000 miles of navigable water. Where it meets the Atlantic, the Amazon is over 200 miles wide, but closer to its Andean headwaters in Peru, it's a more intimate river, and this is where the trips from GreenTracks guide Bill Lamar unfold. The Peruvian Amazon is less impacted by tourism and industry than the Brazilian sections, and for this reason one stands a better chance of seeing some of the rarer flora and fauna. Amazonia, it's worth noting, holds some 70 percent of the world's plant and animal species, including more than 1,000 bird spe-

The Amazon winds some 4,000 miles across South America; this adventure explores the less-traveled Peruvian section near the river's headwaters.

cies, and more than 30 million insect species. On his trip, Bailey checked off 100 kinds of birds, including toucans, macaws, parrots, and parakeets; more than 50 reptiles and amphibians, including whiptail lizards, a black-spotted skink, a red-tailed boa, three calico snakes, a deadly fer-de-lance (the most venomous viper in South America), and a poison dart frog; and plants Bailey had seen only in hotel lobbies—including coffee trees, vanilla orchids, and rubber trees.

The first phase of Lamar's exploration takes place in a canoe and on foot. After traveling four hours up the Amazon from Iquitos in a motorboat, the tour leaves the Amazon for a tributary, the Yarapa River, and a night at the Yacumama Eco Lodge. Yacumama offers guided walks and canoe tours into the surrounding wilderness, which might be adventure enough for most, but for Bill Lamar's trip this is a last taste of civilization. From Yacumama, the group of five transfers to a motorized canoe and pushes upriver. The group stops at will to fish, swim, or hike into the forest. As paths made by the jungle's tribal inhabitants are frequently hunted, most trails are blazed by machete-wielding guides, including a man nicknamed Cosho. "Cosho was given to whipping anacondas out of the water, rousting vampire bats from hollow trees, and bullying tarantulas from their burrows and into his palm," Bailey says, laughing. Lamar and company eschewed tents on this trip, with the night's lodging a foam mattress with a ceiling of mosquito nets and blue tarp. "One night, Cosho whipped up a supper of the most southernly fried chicken I've ever sampled, with plantains, rice, and a blistering salsa made from tiny, freshly picked yellow peppers."

The close-to-the-ground style of exploration favored by Bill Lamar may not appeal to everyone. There will be bugs (some that bite) and rain and snakes and high humidity—which is to say, you'll know you're in the Amazon. For David Bailey, that was the whole idea. "You learn pretty quickly that you don't need all that much to get by," he says. "I started with a list of eighty-two travel items, but only a handful seemed essential: a three-cell flashlight, the antibiotic ciprofloxacin to guard against various gastric ailments, malaria pills, a pair of high-topped, canvas Converse sneakers, and a canteen of Jim Beam bourbon."

> "The only way to garner a measure of control on the Amazon is by first jettisoning any attempt to gain control."

Blue-and-yellow macaws, considered an endangered species, are among the hundreds of bird species you may encounter in the Peruvian Amazon.

20

THE GREAT-APE SAFARI IN RWANDA AND TANZANIA

WHY: See the incredibly humanlike behavior of mountain gorillas and chimpanzees, two of the world's most endangered primates, in the mountain wilderness of central Africa—one of the few places they can be seen.

YOU'RE HIKING THROUGH VERDANT FORESTS WITH BAMBOO TREES and wild celery, and your guide holds up his hand, indicating that you stop. After setting down your backpack and readying your camera, you walk slowly toward the clearing he points to. You reach the edge of the clearing, and there—perhaps only 20 feet away—is a group of mountain gorillas. You're suddenly eye-to-eye with the world's most endangered ape.

"Primate safaris are unique because they can only be done in a few places in the world," says Jeanie Fundora, who has traveled extensively throughout sub-Saharan Africa and the Indian Ocean islands and affectionately calls Africa her second home. "If you're hoping to observe mountain gorillas, your options are even more finite, limited to the Virunga Mountains in Rwanda and Uganda's Bwindi Impenetrable National Park. Volcanoes National Park in Rwanda is the obvious choice for a trip. It's not as strenuous as the Impenetrable Forest, and you're almost guaranteed to see these wonderful animals." (There are no mountain gorillas held in captivity anywhere in the world.)

Volcanoes National Park is the site where naturalist Dian Fossey conducted her research on mountain gorillas; her publicization of their plight very likely helped save the animals from extinction. (Her book about her experiences, *Gorillas in the Mist,* was later made into the movie of the same name.) It's believed that approximately 320 mountain gorillas live in the Virunga range, and 340 in Bwindi.

You'll fly into the capital city of Kigali and settle in at the Kigali Serena, one of Rwanda's top hotels, situated in the city center. The next day you'll rise early for the two-and-a-half-hour drive to Volcanoes National Park headquarters. Not far from Kigali, you'll begin to reach the thickly

A mother and child mountain gorilla in Rwanda's Virunga Mountains.

wooded, mountainous Africa that was among the last parts of the continent to be explored by Europeans, who didn't arrive in the area that comprises Rwanda until 1854. At park headquarters, you'll meet your guides for the day. Park officials will have already dispatched trackers at sunrise to locate the groups of gorillas—there are five or six groups in Volcanoes National Park that are habituated to visitors. Once they've located the groups, the trackers radio back to headquarters with a location. Park officials will assign you to a group of no more than seven or eight clients (there's a limit of fifty-six visitor permits issued a day). "The guides know the family histories of each gorilla group, who the dominant silverback male is, how many babies or young gorillas there are in the group, et cetera. It is as though the guides are extended family of the gorilla families. You sense that these gorillas are a huge part of the life of these men."

The hike to your assigned group of gorillas can be anywhere from half an hour to four hours, and the terrain is striking, very mountainous, with verdant forests of bamboo trees and wild celery. Once you reach the trackers (who stay near the gorilla group once they've been located), you're asked to leave behind any jackets or backpacks. The sound of zippers makes the gorillas anxious, and you don't want them getting angry. You're also told to avoid eye contact with the gorillas, as they may take it as a challenge.

Once you've shed any zippered items and disengaged your flash, you can approach the gorillas with your guide. You're usually within 20 feet. Guests are not allowed to touch the animals, though the babies will often come up and sock you on the leg. You have to stand there and take it, as the mother and males are watching. "My favorite visits are those that have involved groups with younger animals," Fundora says. "In one group, there was a little guy—about eighteen months old, our guide thought—that had hair like the singer Rod Stewart. He went around harassing each adult gorilla in the group, climbing up on the silverbacks' heads, wreaking havoc— much like a human child, if given the chance to misbehave. In that same group, there was a mother with a very new baby. I was straining to see the baby, and she noticed. Finally, she gave me a threatening stare and turned around to shield him from my gaze. It was very apparent that she shared the same maternal instincts as human mothers feel." Recognizing so much of ourselves in the gorillas is a powerful experience and indeed one of the main attractions of this trip.

The next stop on the great-ape safari is the Mahale Mountains in Tanzania, home to the world's largest known population of chimpanzees, estimated at one thousand animals. After flying from Kigali to Arusha, Tanzania, you'll stay overnight at Serena Mountain Village, a lodge set in the midst of a coffee plantation and on Lake Duluti, a sanctuary for 130 bird species. All rooms have private balconies that look out on perpetually snowcapped Mount Kilimanjaro. The next morning you'll take a chartered small plane to Lake Tanganyika, on the border of Tanzania and the Democratic Republic of the Congo, en route to Mahale Mountains National Park.

After you land on a primitive airstrip, a dhow (traditional sailing vessel) will spirit you along the gin-clear lake until Greystoke Mahale appears in the distance, framed by the deep forests of the adjacent national park. Greystoke will be one of the more distinctive dwellings where you've rested your head. The camp's six *bandas*—triangular structures with open fronts and interiors hewn from the timber of old dhows--all look out upon the lake.

Recognizing so much of ourselves in the gorillas is a powerful experience.

The search for Mahale's chimpanzees mirrors the mountain-gorilla trek, but with one big difference: With the chimps, it's not a trek so much as a chase. Once the trackers find the gorillas, they tend to stay put; but the chimps move fast, swinging from tree to tree, and it's hard to keep up with them, especially given the mountainous terrain. You'll hike to the spot where the trackers found them—often by spying the previous night's nests high in the trees or coming upon scraps of half-eaten fruit and fresh dung—only to find that they've moved a mile away by the time you get there. There's no guarantee you'll get to spend time with the chimps, and that's part of the thrill. If you do find them, you'll feel an adrenaline rush; if you miss them, you'll have had a memorable hike and will likely observe some of Mahale's other distinctive primates—including troops of red colobus and blue monkeys.

"People often ask me the difference between seeing the gorillas and the chimps," Fundora says. "I respond that if the gorillas seem like humans, the chimps are even more so. You sense their cunning nature and their intelligence. The hierarchy is very well pronounced. Frankly, I'm more respectful and a bit more nervous around the chimps, perhaps *because* they're so much like us. Every troop has a dominant male. In one group I witnessed, the dominant male had a competitor who was trying to overtake him. Somewhere in his travels, the upstart male came upon a Coke can. He learned that if he banged it on a branch, he could be louder than the dominant male and thus wrest power away. Banging away with his can, he ascended to power—until another chimp took his Coke can away."

Talk about a bully pulpit!

IN THE MOUNTAINS AND THE DESERT

BIBLICAL PROPHETS, ROMANTIC POETS, AND TRANSCENDENTALISTS HAVE LONG SOUGHT SOLACE AND INSPIRATION IN THE OPEN SPACES of the mountains and desert. Modern-day travelers have ample opportunities to do the same. The trips here offer you the opportunity to stretch your legs and mind. They include visits to two off-the-grid destinations—Mongolia and Bhutan—the latter in the company of Buddhist scholar Dr. Robert Thurman. There are several invigorating treks, including the Inca Trail—but on this walk, you'll enjoy the unheard-of amenities of a gourmet chef, hot showers, and staff masseuse.

Travelers who've developed a special passion for a place can open special doors. This is evidenced in Malaka Hilton's tour of Egypt, where guests explore famed archaeological sites with the nation's leading Egyptologist, and dine in the shadow of the Great Pyramids on a meal prepared by a celebrity chef. For those who want to move beyond hiking *among* mountains to scale the peak of a mountain, there's the chance to climb Grand Teton—with the assistance of three of the world's most revered mountaineers.

Sand dunes in Mongolia's Gobi Desert can reach heights of more than 2,500 feet.

21

HIKING THE CANADIAN ROCKIES

WHY: Hike some of the world's most beautiful mountains by day,
enjoy luxurious accommodations at night.

I LIKE TO SAY THAT THE FAIRMONT CHÂTEAU LAKE LOUISE is a four-star resort in a five-star location," says Michael Vincent. A former employee of Parks Canada, he is now Fairmont's heritage interpretive guide. "This is not a slight against the resort but a testament to one of the most beautiful alpine settings in the world—there's a reason that the hotel sits where it does! You walk out of the hotel and you're in the middle of a postcard, with forested hillsides sweeping down to the turquoise waters of the lake and Victoria Glacier gleaming in the distance. Though they share the same name, the American and Canadian Rockies are really very different from a geologic perspective. In Canada, the glaciers have dug valley floors so low that the mountains are that much more dramatic. The vistas are tremendous from the château but only improve when you get out on the trail."

Château Lake Louise is set in Banff National Park, a 2,564-square-mile sanctuary a few hours west of Calgary, stretching along much of the southern section of the province of Alberta's border with British Columbia. The monolithic château is almost the equal of its sensational location, with three sweeping wings spread out along the eastern edge of Lake Louise—a far cry from the tent accommodations you might expect in the middle of the wilderness. The oldest section of the current hotel dates to 1913; the Mount Temple Wing was completed in 2004. Half the rooms look out upon the lake and half upon the forested hillsides; all rooms have elegant stylings harkening back to the hotel's late-Victorian roots. The château boasts a complete health club (including pool) and Aveda spa and a number of dining options, including Tom Wilson Steakhouse, which prepares locally raised Alberta beef and bison.

That the château and nearby Banff Springs Hotel (another Fairmont property) exist in the national park is thanks in large part to the Canadian Pacific Railway and the laws of supply

Visitors can get a close-up perspective of Victoria Glacier (in the background) from a seat in one of Château Lake Louise's trademark red canoes.

and demand; the building of the railroad created a supply of westbound train seats, and the hope was that some recreational centers would create a demand. The original structure at Lake Louise—a log châlet with two bedrooms—was built in 1890 for people interested in mountaineering. This and several subsequent châlets burned down, giving way to the current hotel; modern guests can reach Lake Louise by train or by car. In 1899 several professional Swiss Mountain Guides were hired and brought to Lake Louise to help guests climb the surrounding mountains. The guides were let go in 1954, but in 1997 the notion of having staff guides was reincarnated. Today it's known as the Mountain Heritage Program, and guides lead both hikers and mountain climbers.

One would be hard-pressed to find a richer assortment of day hikes than those originating in the Bow River valley of southern Banff; overall, the park has almost 1,000 miles of trails. Though the château area can be crowded in midsummer, a mile of walking can take you far from people into wild country where grizzly-bear sightings are possible. Yet unlike most wilderness experiences, it's an easy return to the merits of civilization and the comfort of an elegant lodge.

"You walk out of the Château Lake Louise and you're in the middle of a postcard."

The jewel of the extensive trail system around the lake is unquestionably the Plain of Six Glaciers hike. The trail starts out along the lake but soon climbs abruptly; you'll gain 1,000 feet of elevation in the first mile, and this is the toughest part of the hike. "Along the first mile, we talk about grizzly-bear safety," Vincent says. "The Lake Louise area has one of the highest densities of grizzlies in the park, despite all of the sightseers that come to gaze at the scenery. We don't see a bear on every hike, but it's not uncommon—in 2007, I had forty-two sightings. Just knowing that the bears are here is a visceral reminder that we're in a truly wild landscape, and that here people are not the biggest thing in the woods. Talking about the bears also helps distract guests from the altitude gain!"

As the trail levels out, you'll start crossing avalanche paths. The avalanches clear out all the trees, leaving room for new vegetation to grow, which is essential for the pika (a relative of the rabbit), marmot, and other small animals that live here and in turn their predators, like the golden eagle. You'll soon come around a corner and walk into an IMAX film. Behind you is the lake and château, ahead is the Victoria Glacier, thirty stories tall, and beyond that, Mount Aberdeen, Mount Lefroy, and the Mitre (a mountain shaped like a bishop's hat). Not far ahead, you'll come to the Plain of Six Glaciers Tea House. This structure was initially built as a mountaineering hut by the Swiss guides but now is run seasonally by a local family and serves fresh baked goods and tea. "While the teahouse is charming, I like to push ahead to a little lunch spot among some boulders, where we enjoy a picnic lunch that the château has prepared for us. The lunch is nothing remarkable—a good sandwich, some homemade cookies, and pop—but the vista of all six glaciers from our private dining room is first-class: the hanging glaciers on Aberdeen, Lefroy, and Victoria; the Lefroy and Lower Victoria valley glaciers, and the hanging glacier on Pope's Peak. This is also a great spot to view mountain goats, which frequent the talus slopes to the north. After lunch, we'll push along about thirty minutes farther to the Abbott Pass lookout. Here you're tucked right under the glaciers of Mount Victoria, which reaches four thousand feet above you; below there's a two-hundred-foot drop, and shimmering Lake Louise in the distance."

With the long days afforded by a Canadian summer, there's plenty of light left for non-trail activities after your hike concludes at three-thirty or four. A paddle on Lake Louise is a must; the reflection of the lodge's red canoes against the white of the glacier in the lake's trademark turquoise waters is mesmerizing. There's also time for a round of golf at the famed Fairmont Banff Springs Golf Course or a mountain bike ride. If your body is crying for some post-hiking TLC, you can enjoy a hot tub or a massage in the spa. Horseback riding, guided fishing, and whitewater rafting are also available if you desire a break from hiking.

"If visitors are interested in a libation, I always suggest the Lakeview Lounge," Vincent says. "A big Palladian window looks out on Victoria Glacier. If you have a pair of binoculars, you can pinpoint exactly where you were earlier in the day. You'll come away with a grin on your face, knowing that you didn't just *see* Lake Louise, you *experienced* it."

22

A Buddhist Pilgrimage to Bhutan

WHY: The spiritual and cultural wonders of "the Switzerland of the Himalayas"
unfold under the guidance of a Buddhist spiritual leader.

Bhutan is the world's last remaining Tibetan Buddhist kingdom—and one of the most sought-after destinations for trekkers and spiritual sojourners alike. Former *Outside* magazine senior editor Stephanie Pearson had the opportunity to experience the wonders of the Land of the Thunder Dragon with a tour guide uniquely qualified to illuminate the tenets of the Buddhist faith—Buddhist scholar and booster Dr. Robert A. F. Thurman.

"Before I left for Bhutan, I thought that Buddhism was as close to an ideal belief system as you could get," Pearson recalls. "After I returned, I realized that what seems so simple—the notions of selflessness and death that Dr. Thurman lectured on—is in fact quite storied and complicated. But I still think it's a beautiful ideal. And Bhutan is certainly a special place, with its traditional culture largely intact."

Bhutan is a tiny country the size of West Virginia. Tourists were not permitted to visit until 1974, the number of guests is still limited. The Himalayan surroundings are overwhelming. Ancient temples (*dzongs*) cling to hillsides, while towering mountains—including 23,996-foot Chomolhari, "the Mountain of the Goddess"—reach high into the clouds. Perhaps this proximity to the heavens helps lend Bhutan its sacred aura. The significance of Buddhism in Bhutan's culture is constantly reinforced by sights like the multicolored prayer flags fluttering in the wind at Dochu La, a 10,000-foot mountain pass. "In an effort to maintain its cultural heritage, Bhutanese citizens are required to wear traditional dress—at least on weekdays," Pearson says. "For women, that means a kimono-like *kira*. For men, it's a knee-length bathrobe-type outfit called a *gho*."

The tour with Dr. Thurman is conducted with two nineteen-passenger buses traversing the nation's only major highway. American guide Brent Olson (a former resident who has visited

OPPOSITE *Taktsang (Tiger's Nest) monastery clings to a cliffside above Paro Valley.* FOLLOWING PAGES *Buddhist actors performing at Tashichhodzong during the Thimphu Festival in Thimphu, the capital of Bhutan.*

Bhutan more than forty times) provides cultural and naturalist interpretation, while Dr. Thurman handles spiritual navigation. Over the course of fourteen days the group explores sacred temples and monasteries and participates in day hikes, all interspersed with daily meditation and Buddhist teachings. Some of the holy buildings that are visited defy imagination, particularly Tiger's Nest, a three-hundred-year-old monastery. "It perches on a seemingly uninhabitable three-thousand-foot-high cliff, as if plunked down by a divine hand," Pearson says. "From a distance, it's like a mirage—it seems impossible that a building could rest there."

Foreign visitors need special permission to enter Tiger's Nest, which is the home of sixty monks, but entrance is granted if you're with Dr. Thurman. "The dank, cool space was an assault on the senses, like entering somebody else's dream halfway through," Pearson recalls. "Flickering candlelight threw shadows on giant clay Buddhas painted a shimmering gold and lined up behind the altar like benevolent sentinels. On every wall are murals of Buddhas entwined with their consorts in tantric embraces, and the altar is flush with plastic flowers, tarnished coins, butter sculptures, and food offerings."

Perhaps this proximity to the heavens helps lend Bhutan its sacred aura.

Though the government of Bhutan has many safeguards in place to maintain the nation's cultural integrity, modern influences gradually sneak in, and old and new often clash. "On our third day, we stayed in a luxurious hotel in the Paro Valley called Zhiwa Ling—Place of Peace," Pearson says. "It was decked out with a state-of-the-art computer room, and featured Bhutanese-Indian-American-fusion food, satellite television, and bathtubs that would float a small kayak. I learned that when this ultramodern resort opened last September, a reincarnated lama was summoned to perform an ancient 'borrowing ceremony' there. Since all land is owned by spirits, the hotel's owner needed to ask their permission to use the property."

Dr. Thurman's Buddhist teachings are certainly eye-opening, and the beauty of Bhutan's mountains and valleys provides a setting tailor-made for introspection. As Pearson looks back on her trip, one moment seems to crystallize her quest. "Earlier in the trip, I had stood at the turbulent confluence of the Paro and Thimphu Rivers, trying to distinguish where one river begins and the other ends. As I departed Bhutan, I realized that I could either drive myself mad trying to answer this question or let myself be mesmerized by the raucous crash they make as they flow downstream as one. As tenet eighteen in 'The Way of Purification' from *the Teaching of Buddha* states: 'It is hard to attain a peaceful mind.' "

23

THE MYSTERIES OF EGYPT

WHY: Enjoy access to scholars and exclusive exhibits that can't be seen on any other Egyptian excursion.

E GYPT IS ONE OF THOSE DESTINATIONS THAT PEOPLE have heard about since the age of four," Malaka Hilton, *Travel+Leisure*'s most acclaimed Egypt tour guide, says. "By the time they have the means to go, the logistics of the trip might seem daunting. The Mysteries of Egypt excursion was designed to present some of the wonders of the country in a relaxed setting, with some one-of-a-kind embellishments."

After a night at the Four Seasons Cairo at the First Residence, you'll board a private jet and fly to Luxor. Luxor has been called the world's greatest open-air museum and includes many ruins, as well as the Valleys of the Kings and Queens, the final resting place for many pharaohs, their queens, and their children.

On the first night in Luxor, guests are treated to an exclusive dining event at the Medinet Habu temple, the burial temple of Ramses III. Chef Roy Yamaguchi prepares the first of several special dinners on the trip. This feast includes lobster sausage with a cassoulet of Thai-style curried white beans, Chinese-style roasted-duck salad with mango, gremolata-crusted rack of lamb with a red-wine sauce, and a dessert of macadamia tart with green-tea ice cream. All the torches are lit, and spotlights shine on some of the temple's remarkable carvings, which date back to the twelfth century B.C.

The following day, Hilton takes guests to Queen Nefertari's tomb in the Valley of the Queens. "We have a relationship with Dr. Zahi Hawass, one of the world's most celebrated Egyptologists, Hilton explains, "and he's sometimes willing to open the site (which is generally closed to visitors) up for our group." Nefertari was the favored wife of Ramses II, and when she died he commissioned a subterranean tomb festooned with paintings of her likeness by leading artists of the kingdom. "You walk down a shaft, fifteen steps down, and then you enter this brightly colored room, the antechamber. Down another stairway is the burial chamber itself, which is very large. The murals are fabulous, and some of the colors are still remarkably vivid. It's a sight to be seen, made better by the knowledge that very few get to see it."

After leaving the Valley of the Queens, guests board the *Sun Boat IV* for a three-day cruise up the Nile toward Aswan. The *Sun Boat IV* is a five-star vessel refurbished in 2006 with an Art Deco flair. The boat stops in Edfu at the Temple of Horus (the falcon-headed god), one of Egypt's best-preserved temples; you'll also visit Kom Ombo, a double temple honoring Sobek, the crocodile god, and Horus. But there's also pleasure in simply watching the land drift by. "You see people working lush green fields with oxen as they have for hundreds of years, as you sit on the top deck, perhaps sipping a cold Stella beer," Hilton says.

Upon reaching Aswan, the group departs the *Sun Boat IV* for a private plane and flies south to Abu Simbel for a tour of the monolithic rock-cut temples of Ramses II. The highlight here is the four colossi, which depict Ramses II looking stoically ahead with his hands on his thighs. Each statue stands nearly 70 feet tall and measures 18 feet from ear to ear.

Then it's back on the plane and on to Cairo and the Four Seasons Nile Plaza. The next day, guests receive a private tour of the Egyptian Museum with Zahi Hawass and have some time to explore Cairo. The following day, guests get a special insight into modern-day Egypt through a visit with Lady Jehan Sadat, widow of assassinated president Anwar el-Sadat. "We visit Mrs. Sadat in her villa on the banks of the Nile," Hilton says. "She's a very warm person and welcomes us into her living room, which is decorated with antiques and Arabic mosaics; windows look out onto the river. Tea is served, and guests can ask any questions they wish about her life and her husband. When people have asked all their questions, she takes us on a tour of her home. Pictures of her husband with dignitaries from around the world line the walls."

A trip of so many highlights and exclusives could hardly end with a quiet meal at the Four Seasons. "We have a tent set up on the Giza Plateau, with the Pyramids in the background," Hilton says. "We have camels waiting to spirit guests from near the Pyramids across a stretch of desert to the tent. When guests arrive at the tent, a spectacle awaits—a thirty-piece band, a table set with gold chairs and white tablecloths all facing the Pyramids, which are illuminated by spotlights, and attendants on horseback. The Italian designer and winemaker Salvatore Ferragamo is on hand with cases of his most recent vintage from Il Borro estate, Lamelle, a Chardonnay. Chef Roy cooks another remarkable meal.

"The Pyramids remain lit up until our group assembles to go. When the lights go down, just their silhouettes remain. It's as if they are looking back at us."

Outstanding guides—including Dr. Zahi Hawass, secretary general of the Egyptian Supreme Council of Antiquities—make this tour of Egypt shine.

24

In Search of Eagles and Dragons in Mongolia

WHY: The mysteries of Mongolia unfold as you attend the
Golden Eagle Festival in the western mountains and visit famed
paleontology sites in the Gobi Desert.

If westerners have any preconceptions of Mongolia, they generally concern Genghis Khan and the "Mongol hordes," barbarically slashing and burning their way across Asia. The reality of modern-day Mongolia is quite contrary to these visions of its martial past. Mongolians are peaceful people who generally live a nomadic, herder existence, scraping a modest life from this rugged landscape of vast deserts, arid steppes, and lofty mountains. Nomadic Expeditions' In Search of Eagles and Dragons expedition takes guests from the capital of Ulaanbaatar in the northeast to the Altai Mountains in the far west and the Gobi Desert in the south along the China border, exposing visitors to the shifting landscapes of this vast country—and the warmth of its citizenry.

Guests gather in Ulaanbaatar, a city that's undergoing dramatic change. Here you'll find *gers* (traditional Mongol yurt-style dwellings) adjoining modern high-rises. "A few years ago, you could walk across the main boulevard blindfolded," Mongolian cultural ambassador Jalsa Urubshurow says. "Now you'll find yourself dodging Mercedes." After a day touring the city, you'll fly west to the Bayan Olgiy Province near the border of Kazakhstan to attend the annual Golden Eagle Festival. Historically, hunting for small mammals with golden eagles provided hides and pelts as well as food for the people here. Now hunts are done ceremonially.

When the festival is held, eagle hunters come from all over the province, traveling as far as 100 miles on horseback. There's an opening parade, and everyone wears traditional garb—the outfits boast both strikingly bright colors and intricate designs. The competition is held on an open field in a valley surrounded by mountains. One team member takes its eagle up into the

A crescent moon hovers over the gers *of Three Camel Lodge, in the Gobi Desert.*

mountains, and another team member waits in the field on horseback. The eagle hunter on horseback gives a signal, and the eagles are released, racing to land on the rider's arm. Those with the fastest times and best technique are awarded the highest scores. On the second day of competition, the eagles are released from the mountains and swoop down to grab the pelt of a fox that's dragged across the field by a rider; again, eagles are judged on their speed and technique. There are also archery competitions, a tug-of-war, and a review of costumes. Craftspeople sell their goods on blankets around the field, and there's traditional music and even a Kazakh play.

You'll then fly south to the Gobi Desert and Three Camel Lodge. The Gobi is Asia's largest desert, encompassing an area of 500,000 square miles between the Siberian wilderness to the north and the Plateau of Tibet to the south. It's home to a unique assortment of fauna, including Bactrian camels, argali mountain sheep, goitered gazelles, snow leopards, and Gobi bears. The animals that wandered these lands eons ago, however, are of greatest interest to visitors. In 1922, at a site of sandstone formations in the Gobi that have come to be called the Flaming Cliffs, adventurer and naturalist Roy Chapman Andrews became the first man to come upon dinosaur eggs and a dinosaur nest. Many other fossils have been discovered here, and the Flaming Cliffs, just a thirty-minute jeep ride from Three Camel Lodge, are now recognized as one of the world's most prolific and significant dinosaur-fossil sites.

The Flaming Cliffs are now recognized as one of the world's most prolific dinosaur-fossil sites.

You won't be excavating fossils, but leading paleontologists, who may include Dr. Michael Ryan (curator and head of vertebrate paleontology at the Cleveland Museum of Natural History), will help you distinguish dinosaur bones from other species' bones. At dawn and dusk when the sun hits the cliffs right, they give off an amazing red glow against the surrounding grasslands.

The Flaming Cliffs are the first of the wonders that unfold from Three Camel Lodge. One day you'll drive to the west to take in the immense sand dunes of Khongoryn Els, which reach 2,500 feet in height and run some 60 miles north to south. You'll also visit Tugriegiin Shiree, another rich archaeological site where "the Fighting Dinosaurs" (a fossil of a protoceratops and a velociraptor locked in combat) were discovered in the 1970s and where new fossils are regularly uncovered.

The Three Camel Lodge is a small wonder in itself. Guest sleeping quarters are traditional *gers*, based on the tents of nomadic herders, and surround the main lodge, which marries traditional Mongolian Buddhist design and building techniques (all post-and-beam/mortise-and-tenon construction, with not a single nail) with modern sustainable technologies such as solar and wind power. Guests can recline by the lodge's central fireplace or gaze at the desert horizon from a stone terrace or wooden porch while enjoying a libation from Three Camel's full bar. The *gers,* latticed wood structures covered with layers of felt and canvas, are heated by woodstoves and furnished with hand-painted beds. Each *ger* offers unobstructed views of the Gobi.

Though there are barely any settlements anywhere near Three Camel Lodge, a stay there provides a chance to meet local people. "On overland portions of our journey, we stop to visit local herding families who might keep horses, cows, goats, sheep, or camels," Urubshurow says. "If we pass a *ger* and people are around, we'll be welcomed with a warm beverage of green tea, salt, and butter. We'll also receive some dairy product—perhaps *aaruul,* a hardened cheese curd; in the summer, the diet is dairy-based, and most local people have lovely white teeth as a result. If you're invited in for dinner, you might be served *buuz*—dumplings with lamb or mutton, minced with herbs and spices, which is the national dish. If you're visiting in the summer, you might get a drink of *airag*—fermented mare's milk. This alcoholic beverage is a little milder than wine and tastes a bit like sour milk. There's an unwritten code of hospitality in Mongolia, and no visitor is ever turned away. You can stay ten minutes, ten hours, or ten days. In what can be a very inhospitable terrain, this hospitality is also an unwritten code of survival."

While staying at Three Camel Lodge, visitors are encouraged to rise early enough one morning to take in the sunrise. There's a bluff behind the lodge where you'll find petroglyphs dating back fifteen thousand years. When you climb the bluff onto the plateau above, you can see a vast horizon in all directions. At night, stars shine in all their glory. The landscape is lit from above, as there's no light except for the shining stars.

25

HELI-SKIING IN NEW ZEALAND'S SOUTHERN ALPS

WHY: At Blanket Bay you can soar above one of the most beautiful
natural areas on the planet, schuss down through untouched powder,
and land at a luxurious lodge.

PETER JACKSON'S *LORD OF THE RINGS* MOVIE TRILOGY showed the world what most Kiwis already knew—that the Southern Alps on the South Island of New Zealand are an area of incomparable natural beauty. When you drop an intimate, world-class lodge into this unspoiled setting of dark-green forests, snowcapped peaks, foaming waterfalls, crystal-blue lakes, and fjords, you have the makings of an unforgettable retreat.

And that's before you even step into the helicopter for your first off-piste run.

"The sheer acreage available to heli-skiers around Blanket Bay is almost limitless," says Philip Jenkins, luxury hotelier and Blanket Bay's general manager, who settled in the area nearly twenty years ago, in part for the skiing. "The lodge faces the Humboldt Mountains across the lake. To the east lies the Richardson range. With a Eurocopter Squirrel at our disposal, our options are limited only by the weather and skiers' abilities and preferences."

Blanket Bay Lodge sits on 50 acres in the middle of Wyuna Station, a sprawling sheep, deer, and cattle ranch on the northern end of Lake Wakatipu. Since opening in 1999, the lodge has built an award-winning international reputation, for its seclusion, its attention to service, and its accessibility to first-class outdoor activities. The main lodge has eight guest rooms; two free-standing chalets are also available. Each room looks out upon the lake and surrounding mountains and includes a private balcony or terrace. The structure is marked by fantastic attention to detail; to give the lodge a feeling of timeless warmth, the floors have been salvaged from old shearing sheds along the lake and lovingly restored. (Blanket Bay takes its name from the blan-

A helicopter prepares to fly down the mountain so it can return skiers to another run on virgin powder.

kets that were used to create shelters to shield sheepshearers from the elements.) The schist stone used in many of the lodge's walls and fireplaces was quarried locally.

Heli-skiing was pioneered in the Canadian Rockies in 1965 but has only truly taken off in the last decade as enthusiasts seek seldom-skied runs with ample powder and few if any other people. Forget about lift lines—heck, forget about lifts! A whirlybird spirits you off to an unexplored bowl or glacier where the only sound is that of your skis or board cutting through the powder—and eventually the *thuck-thuck-thuck* of your personal gondola descending to carry you to the next virgin run. Blanket Bay selected Southern Lakes Heliski to manage its ski operations; the guides at Southern Lakes have done their homework to identity the fields that have the most consistent dry powder over the seven mountain ranges where they operate. Guests can select the à la carte option and ski by the day or secure the services of their own private helicopter for the length of

A whirlybird spirits you off to an unexplored bowl or glacier where the only sound is that of your skis through the powder.

their stay. There's a maximum ratio of one guide to five skiers; where you go on a given day will depend on snow and weather conditions, your skill level, and how many runs you opt for—two, four, six, or eight. Each run can go from thirty minutes to an hour; when the run's finished, your helicopter is waiting to deliver you to your next spot.

A day of heli-skiing from Blanket Bay might go like this. After takeoff from the staging area (a few minutes' drive from the lodge), your helicopter will head west toward the Tasman Sea, eventually setting down on a ridge in the Humboldts, above Lake Wakatipu. As you ski down, the light gives the snowfield below the look of an infinity pool; it may feel as if you're about to ski off the mountain into the lake, though the lake is thousands of feet away. Near the bottom of the run, one of the guides will have set up a snow table and snow chairs in a sheltered spot with a view out over the lake. A small feast will be spread out—fresh sushi, several salads, cheese and dried fruits, home-baked cookies, and hot chocolate. "On one occasion while my group was having lunch, the pilot flew off to the west coast, purportedly to refuel," Jenkins recalls. "In reality, he set down on the coast near a bay that he knew to hold crayfish—what Americans would call rock lobster. He was back in plenty of time to deliver us to the next run. At the end of the day when he brought us back to the staging area, we opened the ski basket on the skids of the helicopter and discovered six huge crayfish covered in snow. They were on the menu that night!"

Skiing is only the beginning of the outdoor fun around Blanket Bay. The lodge was initially established to provide a retreat for fly fishermen, who make the trek to the South Island to ply nearby rivers for large brown and rainbow trout during the fishing season, from November to May; Lake Wakatipu can be fished year-round. There's excellent guided horseback riding around the large ranch surrounding Blanket Bay, with constant lake and mountain views, and great hiking as well. A favorite way for guests to take in the mountains and glaciers is a jet-boat excursion up the Dart River into Mount Aspiring National Park. Guests who don't opt to ski (or are visiting during warmer months) can still take a heli-tour around the Southern Alps and Fiordland National Park, which has been declared a UNESCO World Heritage Site for its incredible natural beauty. If weather permits, your pilot might fly you over the glaciers and Mitre Peak to Milford Sound, one of the world's most picturesque fjords.

Considering the challenging terrain in the mountains around Blanket Bay, it's quite possible that skiers' muscles might tighten up a bit on the helicopter ride home. There's no need for alarm. "We have masseuses in our spa facility to help guests relax after a day on the slopes," Jenkins promises. "After your massage— or nap, if you choose—we assemble in the great room, with its thirty-foot-high ceilings and grand stone fireplace, for predinner drinks." Dinner is sure to be a fitting conclusion to the ultimate ski day. Blanket Bay has two New Zealand Chefs of the Year on staff. The kitchen emphasizes fresh New Zealand meats and produce -which means an abundance of fine lamb, salmon, and venison. The lodge also takes pride in its Wine Cave, which includes offerings from the Martinborough and Marlborough regions, and the award-winning 2005 Pinot Noir from local producer Amisfield Wines.

26

TREKKING OMAN

WHY: A challenging trek through the rugged al-Hajar Mountains showcases
Oman's natural grandeur and illuminates life on the Arabian Peninsula.

I N TODAY'S POLITICAL CLIMATE, YEMEN AND SAUDI ARABIA might not feel like a
comfortable place to visit for westerners hoping to get a taste of Arabian culture. But Oman,
on the southeastern edge of the Arabian Peninsula, is extremely traveler-friendly. It also happens to offer some brilliant treks, with dramatic scenery and few other hikers. The hiking excursion pioneered by KE Adventure Travel brings you on Oman's finest walking trails and
provides a taste of urban life as well.

The focal point of the trek is the al-Hajar Mountains that run the length of Oman's northern
coastline and rise to heights of almost 10,000 feet above the sparkling waters of the Persian
Gulf. Oman was not open to visitors until 1987, and as a result the remote al-Hajar Mountains
have been viewed by few outsiders. The trails — a combination of mountain tracks used for hundreds of years by shepherds and hunters and paths worn into the rocks over eons by wild animals — are hardly self-evident. "A great deal of effort was put into identifying our route by guides
we've retained in Oman over the years," mountaineer and director of KE Travel Tim Greening
explains. "When you do the route, the first thing that hits you is, 'How the heck could someone
have found these routes?'"

Your Oman expedition begins in the capital city of Muscat, which in terms of ambiance is
about as far away from the rest of Oman as you can get, according to Greening. "It's a sprawling,
linear city, not unlike Los Angeles. There are McDonald's, Western hotels; at first you feel like
you could be anywhere else in the world. But then we visit the Sultan Qaboos Grand Mosque,
which holds the world's largest carpet [over 47,000 square feet], covering the floor of the main
praying hall, and the Muttrah Souk in the old port, where frankincense is burning and all the
vendors are offering you tea. Suddenly you're in Arabia."

The next day you head south out of town in a four-wheel-drive Nissan, toward the moun-

On the Wadi al-Qashah circuit in the al-Hajar Mountains, some of the canyon walls plunge 1,000 feet or more.

tains. On the outskirts of Muscat, the landscape gives way very quickly to desert. The first night's camp is on the Sharaf al-Alamayn Plateau. From here you'll have your first glimpse of the Western Hajar. The lights of the town of al-Hamra twinkle below, a counterpoint to the brilliant stars above.

The al-Hajar are at times austere and imposing, a landscape of jagged ridgelines and intervening canyons parched by the region's hot and arid climate; they bring to mind the sandstone cliffs of Moab, Utah. Hidden among the gaping canyons, which are so wide you must swivel your head to take them all in, are the valleys, or wadis, where much of al-Hajar's human life transpires. Some, watered by springs and *falaj* (aqueduct-like structures that channel water from underground streams or aquifers), support small farms where dates, garlic, scallions, and spring onions are grown for sale in the cities, as well as other vegetables cultivated for village consumption. (Many historians believe the *falaj* were initially built by Romans during their occupation of Oman two millennia past.) Your daily treks will alternate between the ridgelines and wadis, underscoring the contrasting landscape.

> Hidden among the gaping canyons are the valleys, or wadis, where much of al-Hajar's human life transpires.

On the third day, your caravan moves toward Jabal Shams, at 9,833 feet the highest point in Oman. Here you'll take one of the country's most famous treks, the Balcony Route. The path is 20 feet wide. Below are massive drop-offs; above, massive cliffs. Eventually you reach a little abandoned village that's carved into the rocks of the hillside. The village is completely hidden from above and below, and the spot is significantly cooler than its surroundings.

Next you move on to the mountain of Jabal Akhdar and the Wadi al-Qashah circuit. "I rank this as one of the best two-day treks I've ever done," Greening says. "The first day is the hardest one of the trip. The ascent is quite steep, and there's a bit of scrambling involved, but eventually you get up to the rim of a fantastic gorge, and the vistas are worth it." The sandstone walls are a deep, rich red; in some places, huge expanses have a jet-black covering called rock or desert varnish, as if a painter with a 500-foot-wide brush had made a brushstroke. In little patches of soil, delicate gardens cling for survival among the rocks. If you step (carefully!) to the edge, you can look down the canyon walls a thousand feet or more. At times, large vultures—bigger than eagles—can be seen riding the massive thermals.

A highlight of your time on the trail comes each evening, when the light show begins. "What really stands out are the stars," Greening says. "There's no light pollution at all here, and the

Milky Way shines brilliantly. Many guests will drag their sleeping bags and pads out of their tents and sleep under the stars."

Trekking with and among Omanis is a large component of the journey. Most of the guides hail from the villages that you trek through and can explain everything you see, from the ancient juniper trees to the wild "Jesus" donkeys (so named because they are black with a white cross on their backs). The guides' relationships to the villages allow memorable interactions. "During our first day of trekking in Jabal Shams, we came through a narrow gorge with five-hundred-foot sheer walls to the quaint village of Bilad Sayt," Greening says. "An older Omani woman in a very colorful gown greeted us—she is the mother of one of our guides. The father soon came up and invited us to join the men of the family for the 'afternoon social' of eating fresh dates and drinking strong Omani coffee. It's safe to say that in every village in Oman during the afternoon, the men gather to talk, drink coffee, and eat dates. For the next hour, we all sat on old Persian rugs, propped on pillows, talking with the men of the family—brothers, father, grandfather, cousins—with the translation help of our guide, drinking small cups of black strong coffee flavored with cardamom and eating the freshest dates I have ever tasted, from the family's date palms."

Following the trek down from al-Hajar, it's a day of relative indolence in Nizwa, the former capital. If Muscat seems to be heading toward a strip-mall future, Nizwa is grounded in old Arabia. "It's the kind of place where the merchants in the souks don't even take their goods in at night," Greening says. "The people of Nizwa are that honest and trusting." Nizwa craftspeople are especially known for their ornately engraved *khanjars*, the short curved daggers worn by Omani men on ceremonial occasions.

The second two-day trek of the trip takes place in the Eastern Hajar and leads guests along an ancient trading route on the Selma Plateau, ending near the Gulf of Oman. The first day, you are mostly on top of the plateau, with sweeping views of the wadi below and the Hajar Ash Sharqi Mountains. The second day, you drop down through the maze of Wadi Tiwi, which is riddled with canyons—it's a puzzle to make your way down, but the guides know the way. At the bottom you're rewarded with big pools of clear, pure water in the village of Sooee. It's not too cold, and is wonderfully refreshing after eight hours of hiking.

From the pools it's a short walk to your vehicle, which takes you to White Beach, where you'll camp on talcum-powder-soft sand. "The mountains obscure the sunset," Greening says, "but the next morning, the sun rises right out of the sea, a wonderful exclamation point on the trip."

27

Trekking the Inca Trail Like a King

WHY: Enjoy one of the world's great treks to one of the world's greatest historic sites, with unheard-of luxury touches.

Generations of adventurous travelers have longed to look upon Machu Picchu, "the lost city of the Incas." Traditionally, there have been two ways to reach Peru's most venerated attraction: Visitors can take a train from Cuzco or Ollantaytambo (four or two hours respectively), with a range of amenities from bare-bones "backpacker" service to the luxurious *Hiram Bingham* train (with brunch served en route and dinner served on the way back). The other way is to hike in with a trail guide and a few porters. While the latter trip affords you the satisfaction of making the trek under your own power, your camps and cuisine are pretty basic. "I felt certain luxury elements could be brought to the trek to make the camping experience as rich as the ruins," explains Nathaniel Waring, a Peru travel expert recommended by *Travel + Leisure.*

What Waring specifically brings to the Inca Trail is a veritable army of porters—sixty-five for a group of fifteen—capable of transporting amenities like glass- and tableware; Peruvian wines and piscos; an oven for baking fresh bread; and plush tent accommodations. He has recruited a chef from one of Cuzco's better restaurants to up the ante at mealtimes, retained one of the most gifted trail guides to oversee the interpretive elements of the trip, and, in a final stroke of genius and decadence, hired several massage therapists to proffer rubdowns at the conclusion of each day's hike. It's doubtful that Pachacuti, the ruler of the Inca Empire at the time Machu Picchu was constructed, ever traveled quite like this.

The Inca Trail is a walking route that traces sections of several Incan roadways that lead from Cuzco to Machu Picchu, in the Andes of southern Peru. At the height of the Inca Empire, in the late 1400s, there were nearly 14,000 miles of trails crisscrossing South America, a road system stretching from Colombia to the north of Argentina. Some of the paths were 25 feet wide,

The mountain of Huayna Picchu rises above the ruins of Machu Picchu. Twelve hundred people are believed to have lived here in the late 1400s; some residences are shown here.

others barely a yard. The Inca Trail—at least as it is taken by modern-day trekkers—begins at the town of Piscacucho (kilometer 82 of the train excursion) and stretches some 29 miles. It would be an outstanding trek even if the fabled settlement did not wait at the end. The scenery is breathtaking; you'll pass through cloud forests (high-altitude stands of trees that are frequently enveloped in clouds, with ample moisture creating an abundance of moss, orchids, and ferns), along mountains reaching 19,000 feet, and above rain forests and rushing rivers. There are smaller ruins to explore along the way. Distances—averaging around 9 miles a day—are not exceptionally long, but the trail begins at an elevation of nearly 9,000 feet, and some days you'll gain as much as 4,000 feet. Do you have to be in excellent physical condition to trek the Inca Trail? It certainly doesn't hurt, though if you're properly acclimatized to the altitude (best achieved by spending a day or two at elevation before the trek begins), the pace is relaxed enough for individuals of average athleticism to keep up—especially since someone else is doing the heavy lifting.

Guests hit the trail by nine or nine-thirty, carrying just a small day pack for adding or losing a layer of clothing and for water. The porters are in charge of everything else. The group takes its time along the stone-paved trail, lingering at points of interest. Your lead interpretive guide is extremely knowledgeable about Incan history, the day-to-day ways of the people, and the Spanish conquest. Every few miles you'll come across terraced potato fields or ruins of a resting place or temple. "The agriculture of the Incas might not seem that exciting a topic," Waring says. "But it's quite fascinating when you see the terraces there before you and learn that more than two hundred different types of potato were cultivated, micromanaged to the point where one variety is grown on the eastern slope, one on the western slope."

Around noon or one o'clock, you'll come around a corner in the trail to find a dining tent with chairs and tables set up, and big bowls of hot water for washing your face and hands. Your porters have passed you and arrived at the lunch site in time to prepare a hot meal. In the afternoon, you'll trek another two or two and a half hours, and you'll come upon a camp where everything is set up; your duffel bag is in your tent, your sleeping pad and bag are laid out. There's time for a cocktail before dinner is served. The chef strives to combine elements of modern Peruvian cuisine, which is world-class, with the ingredients that were familiar to the Incas—potatoes, chiles, alpaca. The dishes are nicely seasoned and substantial enough to sustain you after a full day of hiking. The massage therapists have a tent set up for massages before and after dinner. Hot showers are also available, thanks to a propane-powered hot-water system.

The trek up the Inca Trail builds in intensity as it approaches its climax. Day one is marked by spectacular views of the immense Vilcanota ridge and 19,134-foot Verónica peak—clouds permitting. Day two serves up the most challenging trekking. As you climb to the top of Abra de Warmiwañusca (Dead Woman's Pass), at 13,776 feet, the alpine landscape gives way to *puna,* dry ground with little vegetation. Domesticated llamas and alpacas are often seen grazing near the top of the pass, feeding on *ichu,* one of the few plants that can grow here. The pass is named not for a dead woman but because the mountains resembled a dead woman to an earlier traveler. As you descend to Pacaymayo Valley and the second night's camp, you'll pass through a cloud forest populated with hummingbirds and other aviana.

Day three may be the most interesting hike of the trip, with a number of archeological sites along the trail. As you approach the mountain pass of Abra de Runkurakay, there's a small oval structure that's believed to have served as a watchtower for Incans guarding the trail to Machu Picchu. Coming down off the pass, you reach Sayacmarca, a village complex with a semicircular construction, enclosures at different levels, narrow streets, liturgical fountains, patios, and irrigation canals. One of the best-preserved sites on the trail is Phuyupatamarca, or Town over the Clouds. From the trail above, there's an excellent perspective of this sacred complex with its fountains. You also get a dramatic view of the descending stone steps that lead to your last camp, at Wiñay Wayna; here the handiwork of the trail is a marvel unto itself.

There is debate in archaeological circles regarding the role that Machu Picchu played in Incan society. Early hypotheses forwarded the notion of the citadel as a spiritual center. More recent theories have proposed that Pachacuti had the city built as a vacation retreat. Nearly as remarkable as Machu Picchu's mountain setting and polished-stone construction is the fact that it exists at all, as Pizarro and his fellow Spaniards laid waste to a majority of Incan structures—and actively searched for Machu Picchu, believing it to contain untold riches. On the last morning of your trek, you'll experience the discovery that evaded Pizarro nearly five hundred years ago.

"We'll get up at four A.M, have breakfast, and hit the trail," Waring says. "We want to reach Intipunku, the Gate of the Sun, for the sunrise. The trail here is on flat stones, along the edges of jungle habitat. When you reach the Gate of the Sun, you're well above Machu Picchu. If you're lucky and get a cloudless sky, you can watch the first rays of sun hit the citadel. It's a fitting reward for what you've achieved."

28

COASTING ON THE KING'S TRAIL OF SWEDEN

WHY: Nordic skiing on the King's Trail in Swedish Lapland brings you splendid
isolation in the pristine wilderness above the Arctic Circle.

L IFE IS NEVER ESPECIALLY HECTIC IN THE NORTH of Sweden, far above the Arctic
Circle. When the valleys and mountains of the region known as Swedish Lapland (or Sápmi)
are cloaked in snow during the long winter season, it's especially still and quiet. Indeed, the
sound of your cross-country skis sliding along in the tracks of your companions—and of your
steady breathing as you engage in this invigorating aerobic activity—may be all you hear as
you make your way under brilliant blue early-spring skies along the fabled Kungsleden, or
King's Trail.

In late March and early April, KE Adventure Travel leads guests on a 54-mile self-powered
journey along the King's Trail. An arctic hut is your home for this icy odyssey—or more accu-
rately, five different huts, each maintained by the Swedish Touring Federation. (Trips are run in
February and early March, but these are recommended only for seasoned skiers, as a faster pace
must be kept to get from hut to hut during limited daylight.) "Though I'm an experienced downhill skier, I had never done any cross-country skiing," fanatical skier Eileen Howe says. "The
way the trip is put together, there's a day to practice with the assistance of the guides who accompany you on the trail. I found that going uphill posed no problem at all; going downhill with
no fixed heel took a little extra technique. The trail, however, has no significant ascents or de-
scents. And of course, we didn't have to carry our food and sleeping bags. We had dog teams for
that." This is a part of the world where dog teams are not a novelty but a practical transportation option. For a group of twelve skiers, three sleds, each pulled by a team of ten Siberian hus-
kies and led by one musher, are used. "The dogs seem extremely intelligent," Howe adds, "and
are very obedient. One command from their musher, and they spring into action."

OPPOSITE *Every element of the Ice Hotel—walls, beds, objets d'art—is sculpted from snow and ice. Temperatures stay at a
balmy 20 degrees Fahrenheit no matter how cold it is outside.* FOLLOWING PAGES *Arctic huts positioned every 8 to 10 miles
provide cozy lodgings for skiers on the King's Trail. Visitors may even be treated to a show of the northern lights.*

The King's Trail runs 265 miles north to south, not far from the Norwegian border; it begins in Abisko National Park and terminates near the town of Hemavan. It was not created by or for Swedish royalty but instead gained its sobriquet from its reputation among aficionados as a "king among trails." After the warm-up day in Abisko National Park, you'll pass through the wooden gateway that marks the beginning of the trail. The route is clearly marked by slender posts topped with red crosses, positioned every 50 meters; this Scandinavian meticulousness may seem like overkill in April, but in the midst of a midwinter blizzard, it can mean survival. The 9-mile course on day one is fairly flat and ends with a crossing of frozen Abisko Lake; you'll learn in the course of the trip that frozen rivers and lakes provide the flattest and hence easiest gliding.

Once you settle into Abiskojaure Hut, your group breaks into smaller teams. "Each team has a task," Howe says. "One team gathers and prepares firewood, one gathers water, one cooks dinner, and one washes dishes. Getting water involves going to an ice hole in a nearby lake or river with a container on a small sled, breaking through the ice, loading the containers, and towing it back. It makes you appreciate running water." This is the routine each afternoon as you reach your hut; the sense of self-reliance this excursion affords you is a big part of the experience.

The huts along the trail are modest but comfortable wooden structures and include sleeping rooms (with bunk beds), a common room, and a kitchen. Each room is also equipped with a wood-burning stove; outside are a well-stocked woodshed as well as an outhouse and the living quarters of the *stugvard,* the hut's volunteer caretaker. "When you reach each hut, you light a fire in the common room," Howe says, "and it's soon warm enough to walk around in shorts and a T-shirt." (How cold was it outside? you might ask. "Comfortable enough to lose a layer when you're moving along," Howe says, "but cold enough that you'd want your down jacket back on when you stopped for lunch, even if hot soup was on the menu.")

After your gentle entrée on day one, you'll begin to ski a slightly more challenging course—but your visual rewards are commensurate with any additional effort you expend. The spreading, undulating terrain of each valley has been likened to a seascape, with snowdrifts and half-exposed hillsides substituting for whitecaps and islands. The long white expanses gain dimension from the snowy peaks that begin to appear on day two as you enter the Ales valley; it's not a landscape of jaw-droppingly stunning vistas, but the trail has an austere appeal that's enhanced by your solitude. You'll climb 1,300 feet in the morning on day two, but the bare expanses of Ales Lake appear in the afternoon, providing an easy finale. At the Alesjaure Mountain Hut complex, you'll find the first of several saunas along the trail. The dry warmth is a well-deserved reward. You'll have the added satisfaction of stoking the sauna's fire and fetching the requisite water; making your own sauna, you can feel entitled to stay in as long as you wish! Dinner in the huts emphasizes sustenance over elegance. "The guides arrange what we're eating each night," Howe says. "We have a lot of pastas, dried fruit. It's nothing very elaborate but hits the spot after a day of exercise." The evening might end with a finger or two of Swedish vodka around the stove.

The wilderness of northern Norrbotten is home to an abundance of animal life, including brown bear, moose, wolf, and wolverine. The animals you're most likely to encounter, however, are the iconic ungulate of the Arctic, the reindeer. In the summer, reindeer feed on grass and leaves; in the winter they feed on lichens clinging to spruce trees and shrubs but mostly subsist on fat reserves. Most of the reindeer skiers encounter on the King's Trail are semidomesticated, herded by the Sami, the indigenous people of Swedish Lapland. Somewhat ironically, the only intrusion of modernity upon Kungsleden sojourners may be the whine of snow machines, which the Sami are permitted to use (by special provision) to mind their herds.

The last few days on the King's Trail settle into an easy routine. The route levels out and the scenery reaches a dramatic climax as Kebnekaise, Sweden's highest peak at 6,945 feet, sweeps into view on the final day. At Kebnekaise Mountain Station, hot showers, plush chairs, and a full bar await you. These creature comforts may be welcome after five days on the trail. But the next morning as a snowmobile speeds you across the surface of Ladtjo Lake to the trailhead at Nikkaluokta, you may think back to the peace and solitude of the Kungsleden – just the blue of the sky, the white of the snowy hills, and the quiet slide of your skis.

If time allows, a special exclamation point on your tour of the King's Trail is a night at the Ice Hotel, in the town of Jukkasjärvi near the end of the trail. Your accommodations here—from the room itself (a highly stylized igloo of sorts) to the bed and accompanying sculptures—are formed from snow and ice that's harvested from the nearby Torne River. No matter how cold it might be outside, the rooms at the Ice Hotel maintain a temperature that hovers around 20 degrees Fahrenheit. Guests climb into long underwear, don a hat, zip into a thick down sleeping bag, and retire atop the reindeer skins that serve as a mattress—that is, ice—pad. The hotel is fashioned anew each December and opens to visitors in January. It closes in mid-April during the spring thaw.

29

SCALING GRAND TETON, WYOMING

WHY: Experience the thrill of a mountain ascent with world-class mountaineers and without the risk and effort of a Himalayan climb.

CLIMBING A MOUNTAIN—A *REAL* MOUNTAIN that brushes the clouds and requires ropes and carabiners and involves at least an element of danger—is a feat that many weekend athletes dream of achieving. But mounting an expedition to K2 or Everest involves a great deal of commitment in terms of time and money, not to mention risk.

Thanks to the nonprofit organization International Campaign for Tibet, you can have a first-class mountain-climbing experience in the United States, hosted by some of the world's leading mountaineers. "We were looking for a way to raise money for the Rowell Fund, which awards grants to Tibetans making contributions to their society and culture," say John Ackerly, president of the International Campaign for Tibet. "One of our advisors suggested an ascent in Yosemite with some famous climbers. When we bounced this off the climbers, they said, 'We'll do it on Grand Teton.' I said, 'Grand Teton it is.'"

Your climbing accompanists include David Breashears, the first American to reach the summit of Everest twice (he's summited the mountain five times) and the winner of four Emmy Awards for his cinematography; Jimmy Chin, a wunderkind adventure photojournalist whose work was recently recognized by National Geographic and Microsoft with an Emerging Explorers grant; and Conrad Anker, renowned for his ascents in the Himalayas and Antarctica and for his role in finding the remains of British climber George Mallory on Everest. "If you're a climber or subscribe to *Outside,* you know who these guys are," Ackerly says. "Some people want to sign up just for the chance to climb next to them."

The Grand Tetons, just north of Jackson, Wyoming, are not America's tallest mountains, though they may be its most recognizable. Rising abruptly from the valley floor, the distinctive jagged peaks of the compact Tetons Range are iconic of the American West. The range boosts at least twelve peaks eclipsing 12,000 feet that climbers can ascend; the big dog here, however,

When climbers reach the summit of Grand Teton (at 13,770 feet), they can view fourteen mountain ranges in four states.

is Grand Teton itself, which reaches 13,770 feet at its summit. "When people see Grand Teton as they fly into the Jackson airport, their first response is 'There's no way we'll make it!'" Ackerly says. "In truth, the mountain is very doable. We've had people show up who've never touched a rope, and people who aren't in great physical shape. One fellow who tackled the climb with us recently had a pretty good potbelly on him but had a great attitude. He was sore as he could be the day after the climb, but he had the determination to do it. Physical attributes don't matter as much as what's in your head and heart. There's also a very tangible team spirit to this climb, the sense that we're all in it together, which gives everyone lots of confidence and support."

One of the special aspects of the Grand Teton climb is the chance to get a crash course in climbing from some of the best climbers in the world. The evening of the day that people fly in, you meet at the home of a Jackson resident who's been very supportive of Campaign for Tibet's efforts. David Breashears is an amateur chef, and he cooks up a meal for everyone, and he and Jimmy Chin each do a slide show on mountaineering and handle some Q & A. There's also a presentation on the plight of Tibet. "A mountain is a challenge and requires determination and fortitude, and the situation in Tibet is a metaphor for that," Breashears has said. "The Chinese are a tremendous force in Tibet. They're fairly immovable and determined, but a determined group of people can take on a foe like that and make a change if they're resourceful and resilient."

The next day, the group—generally five or six guest climbers plus the professional volunteers—team up with several climbers from Jackson Hole Mountain Guides, who provide logistical support for the ascent. Everyone gets fitted for helmets and harnesses, and then it's off to the trailhead and the hike up to your base at Corbet High Camp. The first three hours to a spot called Lupine Meadows are pretty mellow. After a lunch break, the hike becomes a little more strenuous, and the group arrives by four or five. Some steaks are packed in for a barbecue. After dinner the group does some practice climbing using etriers—ladders made of rubber webbing. "The setting of the camp is spectacular," Ackerly says. "The angle where the camp rests showcases the spires to the left, and the lighting is sensational—it's a kind of alpine glow."

The next day, the pros work to get everyone comfortable with the technical aspects of rock climbing at a spot called Garnet Towers. The guides perform a maneuver and then guests follow suit. Preparations include at least one multi-pitch climb and rappel. In addition to practicing the skills necessary to make the ascent, guests get acclimatized to the altitude and build a rapport with and confidence in their guides. When you're rappeling off into space, you have to have a high level of trust in the person manning the rope. Spending time together engenders such faith. For would-be mountain climbers, mastering belaying techniques (managing the rope while someone else rappels) alongside Breashears, Chin, and Ankers is the equivalent of a golfer spending a few hours on the practice range with Tiger Woods, Phil Mickelson, and Lorena Ochoa. "One thing that always amazes me is how well integrated we are after a few days," Ackerly adds. "The world-class climbers are just part of the team." That night, everyone organizes the equipment and guests are encouraged to get to bed as early as possible, as they'll be getting up the next day at 2 or 3 A.M. to start the climb.

"It's usually below freezing when we start, and we get all bundled up," Ackerly says. "It's about three hours of steep walking on loose rocks the first stretch, and you have to be careful not to kick rocks down on the climbers below—though we're all wearing our helmets. Within a half hour of starting out, we're shedding our first layer. By dawn we're up pretty high—the sweeping views out over the valley are awesome. Not long after sunrise, the serious climbing begins. We break into little groups of three or four to tackle the final head wall, which has five or six pitches [sections]. Guests are a little nervous at this point, but psyched too. We always have one of our beneficiaries from Tibet along with us. Their tales of life in Tibet under Chinese rule often provide the inspiration our climbers need to overcome any anxieties. [One recent guest was a young nun named Ngawang Sangdrol, who was arrested for a peaceful protest and spent eleven years in prison.] By the time we've made the head wall, all the other mountains are below us. From here, it's only a few hundred feet more of easy scrambling, and we're on the summit by ten or eleven A.M. If the weather is clear, we can stay a few hours to take in the view—fourteen different mountain ranges in four states!

"The scariest part of the whole climb is the free rappel off the head wall. It's a full 150 feet; you have to launch yourself out into space, and when you do so, you start spinning around. There's no way to prepare guests for it. I've done it many times, but I still get a little nervous. [It certainly helps to have a climber like Breashears as your belay person!] After everyone has landed, you scramble down some gulleys, and then all the way down to the trailhead. It's an extreme day—almost three thousand feet up, and then seven thousand feet down. But it's completely worth it. The elation that guests feel when they've reached the summit—something that they didn't think they could do—is priceless."

IN THE COUNTRY

*C*OUNTRY CAN HAVE SEVERAL MEANINGS. IT CAN MEAN REMOVED FROM URBANITY OR IMPLY A CERTAIN RELAXED STATE OF MIND. IN the context of this section it means both.

These trips transport you from the rugged links land of Great Britain (where golfers have the chance to play all nine courses of the British Open) to the verdant Winelands region outside of Cape Town, an oenophile's delight. A few of these trips highlight treasured destinations like Provence and Tuscany but with a twist; you'll tour by bike (Provence) and horseback (Tuscany), slowing your pace to the gentle rhythm of the countryside. A few take you off the beaten track to take in natural wonders ("The Fairy Chimneys of Cappadocia" in central Turkey) or man-made landmarks ("The Painted Monasteries of Romania"). If you've marveled at polar bears on PBS specials, you'll want to head north to Churchill, Manitoba, to experience the giant bears' annual migration ("Polar Bear Safari"); if you've ever hankered to be a guitar hero, you'll find the right teachers at the ultimate guitar camp, Fur Peace Ranch, in southeastern Ohio.

Snæfellsnes Peninsula and its namesake Snæfellsjökull glacier were the inspiration for Jules Verne's Journey to the Center of the Earth.

30

OF ISLANDS AND OUTBACK

WHY: The incredible breadth of Australia's natural terrain—from temperate forests
to arid highlands to tropical isles—unfolds on this luxurious, private jet tour.

SYDNEY, WITH ITS ICONIC OPERA HOUSE, PRISTINE HARBOR, and casual cosmo-politan vibe, continues to be Australia's top travel destination. But there is more to Australia. When Aussie native Ian Swain set out to create the "ultimate Australia" adventure for his clients, he wanted to introduce them to some of his homeland's lesser-known—but certainly not lesser—treasures.

Lilianfels, overlooking the Three Sisters rock formation across the Jamison Valley, is one of the most highly regarded boutique hotels in the southern hemisphere, offering an English country-house setting with each of the eighty-five rooms adorned in sumptuous floral designs. One could be quite content to sit back and drink in the expansive views of the valley through the delicate blue haze (resulting from a vapor of oil released from dense stands of eucalyptus trees), but the valleys that surround the region beckon you to explore.

Tim Tranter, a local naturalist, conducts eco-tours in the region. One hike Tranter leads is the Grand Canyon walk, which takes visitors through a variety of ecosystems—from dry bush to eucalyptus rain forest—in a matter of minutes. He's well-versed in both the cultural and natural history of the area, and can point out caves where Aborigines lived in the early twentieth century. Kangaroo sightings are possible in the course of your tour of the canyons and rain forest of this World Heritage area, but they are a foregone conclusion at your next stop—Kangaroo Island, which you'll reach by private plane from Sydney.

Kangaroo Island rests just southwest of the city of Adelaide, 10 miles from the mainland. Roughly the size of Singapore, one-third of the island is given over to national parks and conservation areas; this provides fantastic opportunities for visitors to see many of Australia's signature mammals, including kangaroos, koalas, wombats, and wallabies, in the wild. You'll travel to different sections of the island in a four-wheel-drive vehicle and walk into promising habitats

The luxurious guest tents at Longitude 131° all have views of Ayers Rock (Uluru), sacred to the region's Aboriginal people.

with your guide. When you come upon kangaroos, you'll be surprised at how fast they can hop (approaching 40 miles per hour for short bursts) and how high they can jump (7 feet). Visitors are also mesmerized by the koalas that are commonly found in the red gum forest of the Cygnet River Valley. They spend much of each day sleeping, making them an easy viewing target.

Your accommodation on Kangaroo Island is the recently opened Southern Ocean Lodge, set between Flinders Chase and Cape Bougher/Kelly Hill National Parks. Each of the lodge's twenty-one suites features a sunken lounge, a glass-walled bathroom, and an outdoor terrace looking out on the surrounding coastline cliffs. Design elements that speak to Kangaroo Island's pristine natural setting include sandblasted limestone floors and walls fashioned from the recycled wood of spotted gum trees. The Southern Ocean surrounding the lodge looks inviting for a swim, but you'd be well advised to opt for the pool; the presence of many sea lions attracts great white sharks to these waters.

The blinds can be raised with a flick of a switch at dawn to reveal unrivaled views of Ayers Rock.

With your first Aussie island of this adventure under your belt, it's now time to begin exploration of the great interior. Boarding your private flight, you'll start toward Uluru (Ayers Rock). Midway, however, your plane will land on a remote landing strip for a quick tour of Wilpena Pound, a spectacular crater of 52 square miles carved from the arid Flinders Range. The Pound, with its vibrant flora, is quite popular with bushwalkers, but your itinerary will allow only a brief tour by 4×4 and a picnic lunch before you'll reboard your plane and fly farther into the Outback, to the tent camp of Longitude 131°. "Tent camp" is technically accurate—but the tents here will rival many fine hotels. Each luxury tent offers air-conditioning, a private bath, telephone, and mini bar among its amenities. The blinds that close at night can be raised with a flick of a switch at dawn to reveal unrivaled views of Ayers Rock, or Uluru, the iconic Outback sandstone formation that's sacred to the region's Aboriginal people. "You only have to lift your head from your pillow to take in Uluru at dawn," Swain says, "and you can watch the colors change as the sun rises higher in the sky." Longitude 131° offers a number of tours to illuminate the spiritual significance of Uluru and Kata Tjuta National Park for the local Anangu people.

Another highlight is a starlight dinner. You'll head out to a sand dune just before sunset, where tables are set up. After lingering over champagne and canapés as the sun sets on Uluru, you'll dine on a three-course dinner by torchlight right on the dune. Dinner might feature a first-course pan-roasted yellow tail kingfish, crispy skin pork belly with nashi pear purée, and a dessert of banana and caramel tarte tatin; each course is highlighted with fine Australian and New Zealand wines. After dishes are cleared away, the torches and cooking fires are turned off, and a local astronomer takes you through the various constellations in the southern skies, including the Southern Cross.

From Uluru, you will head northeast across the Outback, en route to Wrotham Park Lodge. Wrotham Park is set on an escarpment above the Mitchell River in the midst of a working 1.5-million-acre station (ranch in Aussie parlance) with 35,000 head of Brahmin cattle; think upscale Australian dude ranch. You can visit the working sections of the station to see cattle mustering (a roundup) or tagging, or tour the outlying segments of the property by horseback or ATV. At dusk, you can sit out on the deck of the old sheep shearers' cabins (that have been transformed into luxurious guest cottages, with deep leather armchairs) with a cigar or glass of red wine and watch the river below as the setting sun dances off the rocks.

The next stop on your clockwise tour of eastern Australia is Voyagers resort on Lizard Island, the Great Barrier Reef's northernmost—and most exclusive—property. "The flight out to Lizard Island is an experience in itself," Swain says. "You fly low over the rain forest that rests between Wrotham Park and the coast, and continue at a level of just 500 feet above the Coral Sea. The plane has bubble windows, so you can look down and make out the coral formations on Ribbon Reef as we pass over." Each of the forty villas at Lizard Island looks out upon the ocean or beach; from some villas, you can grab your snorkel and be among the coral in a minute.

Lizard Island is geared toward water sports enthusiasts; activities include world-class sport fishing (black marlin season is in the fall), scuba diving, and exploring the island's twenty-four private beaches. "When I'm there, I love to rise early and hike to Cook's Look," Swain says, "where you get the same views that Captain James Cook did in 1770 when he climbed this rock so he might locate a safe route out of the reefs. After returning to the resort for breakfast, you get a picnic lunch and take off in a dinghy to find a beach for the day. There's a rule on Lizard Island—when you reach an unoccupied beach, it's *your* beach for the day if you want it."

31

PLAYING THE COURSES OF THE BRITISH OPEN

WHY: This tour lets you experience the courses where one of the world's great
sporting events unfolds, just as the pros experience them.

GOLFERS KNOW THAT YOU CAN'T SHOW UP AT Augusta National or Shinnecock Hills Golf Club and expect to tee it up. Entrée to these courses, the site of the Masters and a frequent venue for the U.S. Open respectively, is more guarded than the sanctums of many heads of state.

The classic links courses in England and Scotland where the British Open unfolds are a different story. With a bit of planning, mere golf mortals may play St. Andrews or Carnoustie or Royal St. George's. Or they can leave the planning to Bill Hogan, who serves on *Golf Magazine*'s Top 100 Courses ranking panel, and play *all nine courses* on the British Open rota on a ten-day pilgrimage that promises to connect linksters to the heart and heritage of the game.

Your British Open tour begins in London. "The four English courses on the rota range from the long, windy, and often brutal links of Royal St. George's to the shorter, precision-oriented Royal Lytham & St. Annes," Hogan explains. "Royal St. George's, which hosted the 2003 Open (and will be host again in 2011), is southeast of London, on the English Channel. It's a quirky layout with more than a few blind shots and funny bounces; players either love it or hate it."

Next, it's on to the northwest coast and the town of Southport, home for the next three nights. From here, you'll play Royal Birkdale, Royal Liverpool, and Royal Lytham & St. Annes. Of these courses, Royal Birkdale stands out as one of the most pleasurable walks in links golf. There are very few places where you can see any other holes; it's up-and-down dunes, valleys, and swales. "As you come up through a dunes passageway to a green or tee, you find yourself saying again and again, 'Gosh, that's beautiful,' " according to Hogan. "While the course at Royal Liverpool may not be as interesting as some of the other layouts, the clubhouse is among the most beautiful and well appointed anywhere in Europe, with a treasure trove of golf memorabilia."

From Southport, your foursome heads north to the Westin Turnberry Resort, on Scotland's

A bagpiper signals the day's end at Turnberry.

west coast. In front of the hotel is the Ailsa Course, one of Scotland's most beloved links. "After your round," Hogan suggests, "be sure to visit the bar, order a single-malt scotch, and step outside. Look out over the North Channel to Ailsa Craig as the sun sets, and listen to the bagpiper play. If that doesn't move a golfer's soul, nothing will."

From Turnberry, it's on up the coast to Royal Troon, which dates back to 1878. Royal Troon is so close to the sea, sand blows onto the first fairway. Many times, you'll play Troon in the morning and then play Old Prestwick, a venerable links course in its own right, in the afternoon, as it's right next door. (The very first Open Championship was held at Old Prestwick in 1860.)

You'll cross over to the east coast and play Scotland's most exclusive club, the Honorable Company of Edinburgh Golfers (which most know as Muirfield). "Muirfield is a classic links, with one exception," Hogan explains. "Where links courses generally have nine holes out in one direction and nine holes back in the other, Muirfield has two loops. That means the wind is at a different angle on every hole. One of the highlights of visiting Muirfield is having lunch in the club's famous dining room." With its hardwood walls, chandeliers, and a waiter carving roast beef, the dining room seems to have sprung from Victorian times.

After a round at Carnoustie, the tour bends south again to the last stop—the Old Course at St. Andrews, the world's oldest golf course and, to most minds, the home of golf. "When you step onto the first tee at the Old Course, you feel the eyes of everyone at the Royal and Ancient Golf Club watching you—and the eyes of all the many generations of champions that have played there the last five hundred plus years," Hogan says. "When the starter says, 'Play away,' you feel the butterflies, no matter how much golf you've played and where you've played before." The Old Course is legend for its undulations, random bunkers, double greens, and impenetrable gorse; every bunker, every swale of sod seems to have a name and a story. That is, of course, a big part of its charm.

"St. Andrews is not the hardest course on the Open rota, but it might very well be the most fun to play," Hogan concludes. "The caddies—most of them older gentlemen who've been at St. Andrews a long time—are extremely entertaining, telling stories about Open tourneys they've caddied in and teaching all the way around the course. As you come up the eighteenth fairway, there might be a hundred people hanging around the green, which borders a public walk. For many players, this might be the first time they've felt the pressure that the PGA guys feel. However you hole out, it's a fitting way to end this British Open pilgrimage."

The Ailsa Course at Turnberry on the west coast of Scotland is one of Scotland's most beloved links and the site of the 2009 British Open.

32

PROVENCE BY BIKE

WHY: The sensual delights of Provence blossom forth on this leisurely,
luxurious cycling tour of southern France.

WITH THE IMMENSITY OF THE REPUTATION THAT PRECEDES it, one wonders how Provence can possibly live up to its mythology and hype," opines Benson Cowan, former president of Butterfield & Robinson. "I went the first time after reading Peter Mayles's *A Year in Provence*. I have to say that despite my reading and anticipation, I was not prepared for the onslaught on my senses. The quality of the light was so fundamentally different from anything I'd ever experienced. It was so thick and rich, bouncing off every surface. Light like this can't help but produce good feelings; it influences how you feel about the rest of the world. And the air has a savory quality, like spice. At first I thought someone was cooking, or that there was a bakery nearby. Then I noticed that along the side of the road there was a profusion of rosemary, thyme, fennel, and other herbs growing wild, filling the air with a delicious, rich aroma. To truly appreciate the light, the scents, and the iconoclastic nature of its people, you need to adjust to the slow pace of Provence. Biking lets you ease into the rhythm of the place and brings all the varied landscapes together. To top it all off, the region offers some of the finest cycling you can hope for."

The luxury biking tour of Provence that Butterfield & Robinson has created begins in Avignon and involves three distinct legs, each with a two-night deluxe-hotel stay. None of the rides is particularly taxing, averaging 31 miles a day, with the option for longer rides. (On the days that you move to a different hotel, your bags are conveyed by van; if any of the climbs are too much, the van can help you uphill.) The first leg spins southwest to the hilltop village of Castillon-du-Gard and your first accommodation, Le Vieux Castillon, which encompasses a cluster of Renaissance-era houses in the center of the village and a stunning view of vineyards.

The second leg continues east to Paradou and Le Hameau des Baux, an eighteenth-century hamlet at the foot of the Alpilles range that was purchased and restored by former Swiss soccer

Fresh lavender captures the aromatic and visual pleasure of Provence and you will see it as you cycle past.

star Jean-Claude Milani. Guests stay in the main house, with its shaded terraces overlooking gardens with olive trees and lavender.

The final leg before returning to Avignon brings you north to Mazan and Château de Mazan, which counts among its former residents the Marquis de Sade. Rooms here open up to private gardens or look out upon the tiled roofs of Mazan.

After familiarizing yourself with your twenty-seven-speed hybrid bike, a smooth-shifting Cannondale custom-made for B&R, you'll find yourself riding through rolling vineyards, their light green interrupted by the violet of undulating fields of lavender or the Technicolor yellow of stands of sunflowers. The bucolic scenery is eventually broken by the monolithic Pont du Gard, a Roman aqueduct built more than two thousand years ago.

Your thoughts will sooner or later wander to food. "The cuisine is simple," Cowan explains, "not as layered and complicated as the food in northern France. Much of what's eaten might be called peasant food, in that it's very local, and there's every effort made to use all parts of the animal and what's in season." Guests might enjoy fresh asparagus, incredible pâtés, flower-wrapped chèvre, spicy olive tapenades, nougat from Monsieur Boyer's celebrated nougaterie. In Saint-Rémy, you might plunder local market stalls to assemble a picnic in the shadow of Roman ruins.

There is time to wander local markets, and each little town has its specialty. You can also linger over local wines. "We sample many wonderful offerings, including Châteauneuf-du-Pape, and my favorite, the Bandol," Cowan says. "They are great summer wines, with hints of spice and effervescence. Sitting over a bottle of Bandol is the surest way to get lost in the romance of Provence." The trip also includes dinner at several Michelin-star restaurants, including Chez Bru in Eygalières and Oustau de Baumaniere in Les Baux.

Guests get a special perspective on the magic light of Provence that first captivated Cowan in a visit to the asylum at Saint-Paul-de-Mausole where Vincent Van Gogh committed himself in 1889 and painted some of his masterworks, including *The Starry Night*. "There is a guide there named Mathilde who has been studying and interpreting Van Gogh's time here for years," Cowan says. "She walks us to the spots in the hospital where Van Gogh looked out on various landscapes—for example, the Alpilles Mountains. She then shows us replications of the paintings of the same landscapes—in this example, *Mountains at Saint-Rémy*. Little has changed."

While each day begins and ends at a preestablished destination, B&R's Provence rides leave plenty of room for improvisation. "Each trip has common elements, but no two are precisely the same," Cowan explains.

33

SAVORING SIENA BY STEED

WHY: Approaching the Chianti region of Italy on horseback opens doors to a
remote and extraordinary piece of northern Italy that visitors seldom experience.

A GREAT APPEAL OF HORSEBACK RIDING AROUND THE COUNTRYSIDE of Siena is
that it is very much in keeping with the tremendous history of the place; you find yourself
riding old Roman roads to walled fortresses like medieval knights. "Coming into someone's
domain on horseback is like being given a passport to the local people's hearts," says equestrian
travel expert Bayard Fox. "It shows you relate to their way of life. It also gets you to out-of-the-
way places that you just wouldn't get to otherwise."

And since you're in Tuscany, when those doors swing open there's usually something good to
eat and drink waiting inside.

The Feast of the Conquerors itinerary immerses you in the life of rural Tuscany, combining
daily horseback rides (that often become ad hoc culinary and wine-tasting tours) with cooking
classes at Castello di Tocchi, a fortified medieval village dating back to the eleventh century that
will be your home. Many connoisseurs of Italy will tell you that while the nation's cities have
their appeal, the soul of the country is found here, among the small hill towns and farmland of
rural Tuscany—though it's a soul that can only be understood by travelers who linger. "There's a
lovely charm in staying in a medieval castle—especially one that's been updated with modern
bathrooms and heat!" Fox says. The overall ambiance of the village makes it easy to imagine that
you've been transported back to medieval Italy.

After settling in at Castello di Tocchi, you'll be introduced to your equine companion for the
week. Many of the horses are of the Lipizzaner breed, an offshoot of the Andalusia and native
to northern Italy/southern Austria. All the horses are well trained and a joy to ride. Their keeper
and the host of the riding tours, Vittorio Cambria, is a delight. Part archaeologist, part gourmand, part horseman, Vittorio speaks perfect English and has a wonderful sense of humor and
deep understanding of the region's history and culture. He loves to eat and drink and is a graceful rider and bon vivant second to none. "Being able to enjoy Vittorio's company over the week,"
Fox says, "is one of the great aspects of this ride; he brings the history of Siena alive."

The scenery for your rides around the Chianti countryside is nothing short of picture-book perfect. Forests of pine, oak, cork, and chestnut give way to steep hills dotted with vineyards, orchards of olive and fig trees, and the occasional millennia-old ruin. One day you'll come upon a seven-hundred-year-old convent or hamlet secreted in a clearing; another, you'll follow the ancient roads connecting the castles that once ruled the republic of Siena. You'll likely ride to San Galgano, a now abandoned Cistercian abbey dating back to the thirteenth century. Up the hill there's a twelfth-century chapel that's still in use today. In its center rests a large rock with a sword thrust in it; legend goes that a knight named Galgano buried the sword there as he renounced his warrior past and took his monk's vows.

A benefit of riding through the middle of Chianti is the omnipresence of little wineries, and guests are invited to stop and taste. For the most part, these wines are not sold outside the region, so you'll find them only here. Guests also get a chance to sample these vintages, including Brunello di Montalcino, one of the region's most celebrated wines, at dinner.

Some rides at Castello di Tocchi last much of the day—with a leisurely picnic lunch in the middle; others may be limited to the morning, so guests can spend the afternoon unveiling some secrets of the Tuscan kitchen, with the help of the Castello's gifted chefs. Classes are demonstration-style, with many chances for guests to participate; you'll focus on dishes that incorporate abundant seasonal ingredients. One afternoon you may visit a local shepherd and learn how ricotta and pecorino cheeses are made from sheep's milk. That night you might make ravioli with his cheeses.

One lunchtime highlight at Castello di Tocchi is a visit to an old hunter's shed in a wild-boar preserve nearby. "It was a rather chilly day on one recent visit, and we'd had an exciting gallop through oak forests," Fox recalls. "Acorns are abundant, and they make excellent food for the boar. Vittorio led us up an old Roman road to the refuge, where there was a small shed and a grizzled old boar hunter with a shotgun over his shoulder. He patrols the grounds to guard the boar from poachers. There was a picnic lunch laid out for us—fabulous wild boar, of course, and a local Chianti. The meal had a supremely warming effect. That's another fine aspect of riding around Siena. You build up an honest appetite, which adds a certain zest to the wonderful food and wine. And you feel much better about indulging—perhaps overindulging!"

Horseback riders will find more than their share of centuries-old ruins around Siena.

34

Exploring Iceland, the Land of Fire and Ice

WHY: Iceland's landscape of thermal springs and glaciers makes it unlike any
other terrain, and this tour—by kayak, horseback, and foot—gives you broad
exposure to this small nation's great wonders.

A merican travelers don't tend to visit Iceland, though it's part of Europe
and considerably closer than other European countries," ventures Cathy Piffath, registered Maine Master Guide and certified kayak instructor.

Iceland is nothing if not dramatic, a land of fire and ice, of stark, treeless landscapes and a rich mythical folklore that's quite alive among Icelanders. The "fire" comes from the island's pronounced geothermal activity, which provides a considerable amount of heat and hot water for Iceland's 300,000-plus residents, and from two dozen active volcanoes. The ice comes from glaciers, which have carved many fjords along Iceland's 3,000-mile coastline, and constitute 11 percent of the nation's landmass. The birch trees that once covered one-third of the island were cut to make way for sheep grazing and, for the most part, have not been replaced. As for myths and sagas, it seems that every landmark has a supernatural as well as a natural story behind it.

Iceland's Snæfellsnes Peninsula is said to have been Jules Verne's inspiration for the portal to the inner world in the novel *Journey to the Center of the Earth,* and this tour of the same name begins here. Snæfellsnes, with its namesake glacier (Snæfellsjökull), lava caves, hot springs, and waterfalls, is a microcosm of Iceland's surreal landscape, a collision of green, black, white, and blue. Many people believe that the Snæfellsnes area rests above magnetic fields possessing mystical healing powers. You'll spend a night here at the Hotel Hellnar, a recipient of the Icelandic Tourist Board's Environmental Award for sustainable lodging practices. The next morning you'll hike up Snæfellsjökull, which offers sweeping views of the Atlantic. Like so many landmarks in Iceland, Snæfellsjökull is linked to legend. In this case, it's the tale of Bardur, the spirit of the

OPPOSITE *The Blue Lagoon, a naturally heated public bath/spa, is one of Iceland's most popular attractions.* FOLLOWING
PAGES *The small villages that dot the rugged Westfjords region are best visited by kayak.*

glacier, who is said to have come here from Norway in the tenth century, eventually to abandon his farm and disappear into the glacier.

Your journey continues on toward the rugged Westfjords, one of Iceland's least populated regions and home to the Látrabjarg bird cliffs — 9 miles of nesting seabirds along the most westerly land in Europe. Atlantic puffins, kittiwakes, fulmars, razorbills, and guillemots in the millions nurture their young here in the late spring and summer. Using Ísafjördhur (the capital of Westfjords) as a base, you'll explore some of the region's many fjords by kayak. "Before going, I expected the Icelandic fjords to be like those in Norway—very steep, plummeting abruptly to the water with no place to get out," Piffath says. "They're not like that at all. The walls of the fjords slope very gradually; in places it's like farmland, and indeed there are horses and sheep grazing near the shore in some fjords. Having so many places to pull out of the water is great for kayaking, as you can easily stop and stretch your legs. Thanks to the shelter from the Atlantic the fjords provide, there are few waves, and the paddling is quite easy."

Next, you'll explore the Hornstrandir Nature Preserve by foot and catch glimpses of the arctic foxes that prowl the hilltops in search of field mice. As your journey winds down, you return (by air) to Reykjavík—a hip, stylish counterpoint to the rustic charms of the fjordlands. While you'll get a taste of Iceland's urban lifestyle, a bit of the Old World awaits just fifteen minutes outside the city—a ride on an Icelandic horse through the lava fields surrounding Mount Helgafell volcano.

En route to the airport, you will take a short detour to the Blue Lagoon, a small manmade lake of naturally heated mineral water among the lava fields that's operated as a large public bath/spa; it's one of Iceland's most popular attractions. "The water in the lagoon varies from hot to very hot," Piffath explains, "and you walk around until you find a place that you're comfortable with. The silica mud in the lagoon is supposed to be great for the skin, and there are buckets of the mud around the lagoon. I put a mud pack on my face and sat back for five minutes. It felt great, and made for a very relaxed plane trip home."

35

FLOATING THE SOUL OF IRELAND

WHY: A luxury barge trip on the River Shannon reveals the tastes, charms, and history of a rural Ireland that's off the beaten path.

THE RIVER SHANNON IS IRELAND'S LONGEST INLAND WATERWAY, flowing over 200 miles through the center of the Emerald Isle. It passes through some of Ireland's most tranquil, scenic landscapes, yet is removed from the tourist centers; it's a setting in which you can experience an Ireland where there's more than lace curtains and leprechauns. There's no better way to savor the pleasures of the River Shannon than from the deck of the *Shannon Princess II,* a luxury barge that slowly makes its way downriver for 125 miles, stopping along the way so you can take in draughts of local lore.

"The *Shannon Princess II* is owned and operated by an Irish couple—Captain Rauiri Gibbons and Olivia Power," says luxury barge expert Amy Aldrich. Rauiri is extremely knowledgeable about the region's history, and Olivia is one of Ireland's more celebrated chefs and at the forefront of New Irish cuisine. Together they have tremendous pride of ownership and are very devoted to providing guests with an experience that reflects the old Ireland and the new."

The *Shannon Princess II* is an excellent example of the kind of luxury barge that travelers may more readily associate with the canals of France. At 105 feet long and 19 feet wide, the barge has a long, narrow profile that allows it to navigate the locks that enable craft to move through shallow sections of the waterway. The boat can accommodate up to ten guests in five cabins. The cabins are small (typical of barge craft), but each has an opening picture window that looks out on the river and an airy en suite bathroom with shower. Much of your waking time on board is spent in the spacious salon, which is comfortably appointed with leather sofas and chairs, and large windows open to the passing scenery. All the linens on board, as well as the crystal and porcelain, are made by local craftspeople.

Your day begins with a breakfast that always includes freshly baked goods—biscuits, scones, gingerbread—and fresh berries (from local fields when in season) and herbs and flowers for the table setting. As guests sip coffee or tea, Captain Rauiri outlines the day's itinerary, and then the cruising begins. Many guests will decamp from breakfast for the sun deck—even if the sun isn't

shining—to take in the vistas of pastoral life. "The Shannon is not all a flowing river but a system of lakes interconnected by sections of river," Rauiri Gibbons explains. "On the first three days of the cruise, it's predominantly river. Fields of grass roll right down to the river's edge, and there are cows, horses, and deer, and farmers cutting and gathering the grass to make hay for their animals. The last few days of the journey the flowing water gives way to lakes that are bounded by hilly country. It's a pleasing contrast."

You won't visit the Blarney Stone as you motor along through the heart of Ireland, but you will have the chance to tour several less-encountered historical sites, and linger at some charming waterside towns. One day a motorcoach will deliver you west to the lively university city of Galway, where you'll take lunch in the Quays Bar, a traditional Guinness and Oyster pub decorated with intricately constructed stained glass, and have an opportunity to peruse fine Irish crystal in adjoining shops. Another day you'll moor at the ruins of Clonmacnoise, originally built as a monastery in A.D. 545 on a hill above the Shannon. Several ancient Celtic crosses carved from sandstone remain largely intact on the site among the ruins.

For Amy Aldrich, the most memorable excursion of the cruise was an afternoon spent at Leap Castle, near the hamlet of Terryglass, which has been described as Ireland's "most absurdly beautiful small village." The castle was initially constructed in 1250, and since that time has been partially destroyed and rebuilt several times. Its current owner is Sean Ryan, who is one of Ireland's foremost tin whistle players. Ryan has been very active in restoring the castle to its former glory. "Sean is there when you visit, and he gives a private tour of the castle, which is reputed to be the most haunted castle in Ireland," Aldrich says. "Sean also plays a few songs for his visitors. If you're lucky, his daughter, Ciara, may be around. She's an award-winning Irish dancer, and will likely perform some jigs and reels as he accompanies her on the whistle."

No matter how beguiling the Shannonside attractions, chef Olivia Power's cuisine is always a good reason to return to the barge. Power focuses her creations on what's fresh and local; most ingredients are sourced from river- or lakeside markets and, in some cases, foraged. In the spring and summer, the menu features many fish dishes—sea bream with marjoram and asparagus, for example. In autumn, more game finds its way onto the menu—wild duck, wild venison, and rabbit. Power makes a special effort to couple great wines with her meals. Of course, you can always treat yourself to a Black Velvet—a cocktail of Guinness stout and champagne.

A guest enjoys breakfast—including chef Olivia Power's freshly baked biscuits and scones—on the sundeck of the Shannon Princess II.

36

Polar Bear Safari in Manitoba

WHY: There is no better place in the world to witness these fearsome
predators in the wild than from Manitoba's Tundra Buggy Lodge.

Come October each year, a portion of Hudson Bay north of Churchill,
Manitoba, begins to freeze over. A precursor of the long winter to come, the gathering ice
also signals the arrival of a stream of visitors that swells the population of this town of fewer
than 1,000 at the edge of the tundra. Most have come to see the Churchill area's famed ursine
visitors in the great polar bear migration.

Given the polar bear's voracious nature, human visitors are forbidden from wandering the
tundra on foot. All polar bear viewing is done from the safety and comfort of a Tundra Buggy, an
exceptional vehicle designed exclusively for traversing these alternately spongy and frozen environs. The length of a school bus, the buggies have a height of nearly 20 feet, with tires that dwarf
those on the average Hummer. The heated buggies can host up to forty passengers, with two
rows of bench seats and a wide aisle in between. There's a small deck in the back where photog-
raphers can set up for shots in the open air.

For the polar bear enthusiasts who make the trip to Churchill (guests generally opt for three-
night stays, which allow for two days on the tundra), there are two accommodation options: You
can stay at a hotel in town and take Tundra Buggy excursions the 15-odd miles out to the Churchill
Wildlife Management Area where most of the bears are; or you can stay in the wildlife area itself
at the Tundra Buggy Lodge. The lodge links together five trailerlike modules resting atop Tundra Buggy tires in a structure that stretches 100 yards and resembles a train. Two of the modules
provide sleeping quarters (with shared bathrooms and showers); one serves as a kitchen/dining
room; one is a lounge; and the other houses utilities and supplies. While the accommodations
and amenities are rather utilitarian, the lodge is certainly comfortable and gives guests a distinct
location advantage over visitors staying in town. "Guests at the lodge have the best possible access to wild polar bears, as you're staying in the middle of their environment," John Gunter ex-

Adolescent male polar bears spar as visitors look on from the comfort and safety of a Tundra Buggy.

plains. He is general manager of Frontiers North Adventures, which has provided cultural, photography, and adventure tours in northern Canada since 1986. "You wake up with polar bears in the periphery, have breakfast with polar bears outside, and can watch bears as the sun sets. You're with the animals before the buggies come out from town and after they leave."

After you've eaten a hearty breakfast, your buggy picks you up by 8 A.M.; this will give you an hour and a half of privacy on the tundra, before the buggies from town arrive. Despite their size and clamor, the Tundra Buggies do not repel the bears. In fact, the bears will sometimes approach the vehicles and stand on their hind legs for a look inside. Though the deck is nearly 14 feet off the ground, large bears have been known to place their outstretched paws on the grating.

As you come upon bears, the buggy will stop so you can watch and photograph them through the glass or from the platform. The buggy then seeks out unique bear interactions, such as a mother sitting up and nursing a cub. With a little luck, you'll be able to witness one of the highlights of a polar bear safari—the sparring of two adolescent males. The bears will stand on their hind legs, fully upright, and begin swatting at each other; the behavior is intended as play. By two-thirty, the town buggies are heading home, and Tundra Buggy Lodge guests have another hour alone with the bears, as well as the purples and reds of the sunset.

When you get back to the lodge, there's a happy hour with hors d'oeuvres, or a chance to grab a nap. The lodge trappings are quite simple, but it's toasty warm inside, a sharp contrast to the outside chill; on a clear night, you might be treated to the northern lights. Dinners feature regional cuisine—wild arctic char or Manitoba elk or beef. After dinner one of the lodge's naturalists gives a lecture on the bear's life cycle, the tundra environment, and the cultures of the local First Nation people.

"When you first lock eyes with a polar bear and it acknowledges you, it's an inspiring experience," Gunter says. "You're making a connection with a wild, solitary animal, an animal that would pose extreme danger if you encountered it outside the buggy. This connection inspires strong reactions. One of our guests this past fall was a woman from Italy who couldn't speak much English. Because of our language barrier, we didn't have many conversations. When she observed a bear just outside the buggy and it looked back at her, tears came into her eyes. She said something in Italian with great passion, grabbed me, and gave me a wet kiss."

37

TO THE NORTH POLE, NORWAY

WHY: Experience the solitude of the upper Arctic and exhilaration of reaching
the top of the world under your own power.

FEW TRAVELERS ARE PREPARED TO MUSH 475 MILES through temperatures of -35 degrees Fahrenheit (and colder) to reach the North Pole as explorer William Peary and his partner Matthew Henson did in 1909—and as Rick Sweitzer did in 1992. Thanks to Sweitzer and the adventure travel company PolarExplorers, you can participate in a miniature North Pole expedition that distills the thrill of reaching the top of the world in the course of a five-day adventure via jet, helicopter, and cross-country skis.

Your expedition begins in Oslo, Norway, with a reception at the Fram Museum, which is devoted to the history of polar exploration. After a night at the Hotel Continental, you'll rise early for a two-and-a-half-hour flight to Longyearbyen, a settlement on the island of Spitsbergen. Spitsbergen is 400 miles north of the northernmost point of the Norwegian mainland (that's 78 degrees north latitude) and 600 miles south of the North Pole; it's the northernmost point in Europe. Though isolated by anyone's standards (the island has been chosen by the Norwegian government to house a doomsday seed bank), Longyearbyen is surprisingly well-appointed with fine lodging and eateries, thanks to the coal mining operations that were established here in the early twentieth century, and to the town's more recent emergence as a gateway to Arctic adventure.

"I call Longyearbyen the Chamonix of the Arctic," polar explorer Rick Sweitzer says. "There are fjords, mountains, and glaciers—all very beautiful—plus a very happening scene. One restaurant—Huset—has the largest wine cellar in all of Norway." You'll stay the night at the Spitsbergen Hotel, built in the 1940s as a mining company headquarters. Dinner will be at the Funktionaermessen Restaurant in the hotel, which looks out over the town and Longyear Glacier. Cuisine here has a French flair, though Arctic specialties such as seal, whale, reindeer, grouse, char, and occasionally polar bear are available for the adventurous palate.

The following day you'll board a chartered Antonov 74 jet to venture farther off the grid to Barneo, a research camp at 89 degrees north latitude—about 60 miles from the Pole, or another

two and half hours from Longyearbyen. "Barneo is maintained as a base camp by the Russian government for three or four weeks a year for researchers and adventurers heading to the Pole," Sweitzer explains. "Its exact geographic location is always shifting—like that of the North Pole itself—as it's a spot on the ice, and the ice is moving. Each year a few people will investigate the general area to find ice that's thick enough to land a plane on—1.65 meters is enough. They'll then parachute a tractor in to smooth out a runway on the ice that can accommodate a jet; it has to be at least a thousand meters in length. The pilots are exceedingly skillful; the landing is so smooth, you can't believe you're landing on a runway carved on ice.

"When you step out of the plane, the cold air slaps you in the face. It almost takes your breath away. There will be a Siberian fellow waiting with a sign in English that says FOLLOW ME; sometimes another guy will be wearing a polar bear suit to greet guests. The camp is four to eight half-dome style tents with wooden doors and kerosene-fired heaters, and a mess tent maintained by a pleasant Ukrainian woman named Galina, who serves hearty food—borscht and salami—and sells beer and whisky as a sideline." After you've deposited your belongings in your tent, you'll go for a test run on your skis, pulling a light sled. Everything but the tents of the camp is white, though pressure ridges (piles of ice created when ice floes expand against one another and swell up) give the expanses some definition. As the day progresses, time becomes a confusing concept; in April (when North Pole expeditions are conducted), there are twenty-four hours of sunlight. "The sun goes along the horizon, but never dips," Sweitzer explains. "All the lines of longitude that define a time zone converge at the top of the world; effectively, you're in all time zones at once. To have a consistent point of reference, we set our watches to Long-yearbyen time."

The following morning you'll make your assault on the Pole. After breakfast you'll climb into a Russian Mi-8 helicopter and be flown within striking distance—generally 10 kilometers away. The helicopter pilot will determine a landing point that will minimize any pressure ridges and open water that the group might have to pass. "We're usually on the ice by noon," Sweitzer says, "and we try to get moving as soon as possible so we can maintain warmth. Guests feel both anticipation and trepidation as we set off on our skis. I think this is because there's such a palpable sense of heading off into the unknown."

The geographic North Pole is a fixed point on the ocean floor, some 12,000 feet below the surface of the Arctic Ocean, but as mentioned before, the ice that covers the surface is constantly

Guests close in on the North Pole, carefully negotiating breaks in the ice. There's no fixed position for the North Pole on the ice, as the ice is constantly moving. A GPS reading lets you know you've reached the top of the world.

moving. Thus, explorers use GPS to locate the Pole, which is 90 degrees north latitude. "There's no straight line to reach the top of the world, as it's always shifting," Sweitzer explains. "Sometimes we'll have to zig east or west or even south to go around pressure ridges or stretches of open water, or to accommodate the drift of the ice. When the GPS reads 89.59, we know we're getting very close, and we'll unhitch the sleds we've been pulling. The group heads left, then right, trying to locate that magical 90 degrees. Finally we find it and click 'Save' on the GPS. We have a good bottle of champagne along and a champagne flute for each guest, and we have a toast and snap a bunch of photos to celebrate. Everywhere you look is south. Everywhere the ice is drifting is south. It's a tough concept to grasp."

"All the lines of longitude that define a time zone converge at the top of the world; effectively, you're in all time zones at once."

That night you and your fellow explorers will pitch tents at the North Pole and enjoy a calorie-laden dinner like fettuccine carbonara; a heavy meal is essential, as your body is churning out heat twenty-four hours a day to maintain your core temperature and needs fuel. You'll sleep two or three to a tent, in a heavy-duty sleeping bag and bivy sack with two sleeping pads between you and the ice. Each tent has a camp stove to supply a bit of extra heat.

"The next morning we'll wake up two to five miles from where we went to sleep, thanks to drifting ice," Sweitzer says. "We'll have a little breakfast, and soon the Mi-8 will touch down to scoop us up. There will be time for some of Galina's hot soup at Barneo before the Antonov 74 lands to bring us back to Longyearbyen, which looks pretty warm after the North Pole. Before the day is out, you'll be enjoying a hot shower at the Spitsbergen Hotel and a drink by the fireplace, while you review your pictures of the top of the world."

38

PICKIN' AT OHIO'S FUR PEACE RANCH

WHY: Guests can hone their guitar skills with some of the world's best players
in an intimate, unpretentious atmosphere.

ROCK 'N' ROLL FANTASY CAMPS HAVE SPRUNG UP stage left and right in recent years, giving air-guitar avatars and assorted wannabes a chance to rub shoulders with slightly past-their-prime rock stars. Fur Peace Ranch, nestled in the rolling hills of southeastern Ohio, offers aspiring guitarists something a bit different. While visitors to the ranch certainly have a chance to share tête-à-têtes with famous guitar slingers (among them Jorma Kaukonen, former lead guitarist of the Jefferson Airplane, Fur Peace's cofounder and proprietor), the emphasis here is on improving your playing. "It's a place to grow guitar players," Kaukonen stated in the ranch's charter.

Bill Thompson has played electric guitar in bands since junior high school (he's currently in the Swinging Orangutans). For him, a visit to Fur Peace Ranch was an opportunity to learn some new licks—and just as important, to see if he still had it. "I saw Fur Peace as a guitar-playing proving grounds," Thompson recalls. "It was like going to a major-league training camp and seeing if you could hit a real fastball. But for all the intensity of the workshop sessions and the presence of some of the world's very best players, the environment is incredibly welcoming and low-key. There are many informal jam sessions in addition to the workshops, and whether or not you're much of a player, you're given lots of encouragement and made to feel like your contribution matters."

The serene countryside of Pomeroy, Ohio, is a far cry from the Haight-Ashbury of 1967, where the Jefferson Airplane—powered by the soaring vocals of Grace Slick and the screaming guitar of Jorma Kaukonen—helped define the psychedelic San Francisco sound. The Airplane eventually disbanded, but Kaukonen and bassist Jack Casady pursued a common affection for country blues, forming the band Hot Tuna, which still performs today. Hot Tuna is fueled by Kaukonen's virtuosic fingerpicking, and students at Fur Peace can study this technique face-to-face with one of its modern masters. Many other guitar legends pass through Fur Peace; a partial list of recent instructors includes Roy Book Binder (who's recorded five solo albums and toured

with B. B. King and Bonnie Raitt), David Bromberg (who in addition to his solo act has contributed to more than one hundred albums for such artists as Bob Dylan, Ringo Starr, and Mississippi John Hurt), Cindy Cashdollar (dobro player extraordinaire, frequent guest on Garrison Keillor's *Prairie Home Companion,* and recent inductee into the Texas Western Swing Hall of Fame), and Bill Thompson's desired instructor—G. E. Smith (former *Saturday Night Live* bandleader and sometime sideman for David Bowie and Bob Dylan).

The log-cabin structures that dot Fur Peace Ranch are reminiscent of summer camps of a bygone era. Or, as Thompson describes, "a hippie farm/commune without all the negative connotations." The lack of in-room entertainment amenities encourages visitors to mix and participate in the ad hoc jam sessions that are an integral part of the experience.

After a brief orientation session ("No drugs, no alcohol, lots of music!") and lunch, students split off to attend their first workshop. After dinner on day one, there's a campfire sing-along session, the most star-studded sing-along you're likely to ever attend. "Jorma is always around and very accessible," Thompson says. "You get the sense that the guest instructors really enjoy being there. They get a chance to recharge their batteries in a low-key setting."

One of the highlights of a plucking-and-picking stay at Fur Peace Ranch comes on Saturday night, when the weekend's instructors play a concert in the two hundred-seat Fur Peace Station, the ranch's concert hall. During Thompson's stay, G. E. Smith played a set with Jack Casady on bass. This was followed by a solo set by Jorma Kaukonen. Another highlight is Sunday afternoon's student concert, where attendees gather to trade some of the new licks they've learned over the weekend. "Each class plays a song as a group," Thompson explains. "Our class got up and played a straight-ahead blues number. When it came time for the first solo, G. E. Smith pointed at me and I took it. I didn't think that things could get much better, but they did. After each of the student groups runs through its numbers, individual students have the chance to go up and play a song. I chose to play a song that I'd written called 'Magnetic,' and G.E. played along with me. I thought that he'd play the leads, but he played rhythm guitar. So there I was, playing one of my own numbers for Jorma Kaukonen and Jack Casady, with G. E. Smith backing me up."

Visiting guitarists study with the world's finest pickers—and jam with one another—at Jorma Kaukonen's Fur Peace Ranch.

39

The Painted Monasteries of Romania

WHY: Experience central European life as it was lived a hundred years ago, as
well as some of the world's greatest biblical frescoes.

Positioned at a critical geographic nexus between the East and the West,
Romania has been the focus of assaults and annexations for the better part of the last millennia. Since the ouster of dictator Nicolae Ceausescu in 1989, an existence marked by political
oppression has gradually improved. So has Romania's appeal as a tourist destination. Thanks to
its political isolation—and the physical isolation imposed by the Carpathian Mountains that
wind through the nation—parts of Romania seem to have been cut off from the twenty-first
century. The Carpathians here hold some of the wildest terrain left in Europe, with populations
of brown bears, wolves, and lynx. Romania's distance from modernity is a large part of its
charm.

"I must admit that I went on my first journey to Romania with many uncertainties," recalls
Anthony Bay, principal European product designer for Abercrombie & Kent. "While the tourist infrastructure was rather basic on my initial visit ten years ago, it's come a long way in a short
amount of time. You'll never find a palace hotel outside of Bucharest, but accommodations are
clean and comfortable. I've led two groups of visitors there now, and I found only great hospitality and a sense of vitality around the villages."

As you tour the countryside of Transylvania, you'll observe that people live especially close to
the land. One of the first things you notice when driving through this rolling countryside in the
foothills of the Carpathians is that all agriculture is done by hand. You'll see people bent double
in the fields, reaping and sowing their crops. There's no clear delineation between fields and
uncultivated land; it's difficult to tell what's being grown and what's being laid to waste. The
food here—served in simple restaurants that cater to locals and, on at least one occasion during
your Abercrombie & Kent–hosted tour, in a local farmhouse—is flavorful (paprika is the spice
of choice), wholesome, and locally sourced. Lots of wild-boar stew is served, as well as loin of

A walk through the walled town of Sighişoara, Transylvania, can easily transport visitors back to medieval times.

pork and soups served with dollops of sour cream. There are very few cars; horse-drawn carriages lumber down the country lanes that connect one medieval village to the next. Most horses will have a red flower affixed to their bridles, a talisman to keep the evil eye at bay.

The medieval villages—including enclaves in the towns of Sighişoara, Sibiu, and Braşov—are one of the great attractions of Transylvania. These villages were constructed largely by Saxons, who were courted to relocate to the region in the twelfth and thirteenth centuries by the ruling Hungarians, who hoped that Saxon military would lend muscle against marauding Tatars. Their architectural style evolved with security in mind; exterior walls surround the larger villages, and even the houses have fortresslike gates and walls. The churches are a central focus of the villages, both for spiritual and defense purposes; it was here that women and children would gather in the case of battle. Sibiu, which was recognized as a European Capital of Culture in 2007, originally had thirty-nine defensive towers and was considered the best-fortified town in Romania. Its twisting cobbled streets take one back to the twelfth century, with the welcome modern addition of a thriving café culture. Sighişoara, a UNESCO World Heritage site, has a fantasy quality; one might think that Hollywood had fabricated this village for a set piece calling for "middle-European castle."

"It is almost impossible to describe the impact of the paintings when you first behold them."

That some of the villages are incredibly intact stems more from indifference than from conscious efforts of preservation. "The Saxon families who'd lived here for many generations returned to Germany when the iron curtain lifted," Bay explains. "Many of the villages were deserted at that time, and some are in danger of being taken over by Gypsy people (who are accepted in Romania but who have shown no inclination toward historic preservation). There's currently an international effort under way to preserve the villages. England's Prince Charles is spearheading this movement, along with writer/artist Jessica Douglas-Home and her nonprofit organization, the Mihai Eminescu Trust."

From Transylvania, a short private flight brings you to the northern reaches of Romania and the region of Bukovina, home of one of Eastern Europe's greatest (and perhaps least-known) cultural relics—the painted monasteries. Bukovina is in mountainous country, even more isolated than Transylvania; it's still very difficult to reach the monasteries, which is why they aren't better known. That also explains why they remain in such pristine condition. These Eastern Orthodox Church monasteries date back to between 1522 and 1547 and were initially constructed as final resting places for nobles and princes. The practice of painting biblical murals was common during this period, with the frescoes serving to elucidate Old and New Testament events to illiterate faithful.

Visitors traveling with Abercrombie & Kent focus their time on three of the monasteries—Humor, Sucevița, and Voroneț, where murals festoon exteriors and interiors. While many biblical stories depicted at each site repeat themselves, the interpretations are nuanced. The monastery at Humor, the Church of the Assumption of the Holy Virgin, was constructed in 1530. Its most striking fresco depicts the Last Judgment, which captures the hand of God weighing souls and Archangel Michael warding off devils. The paintings at the monastery at Sucevița were completed later than those at the other churches, around 1595, and hold more scenes than any of the other monasteries. The Church of Saint George at the Voroneț Monastery may be the most revered church in Romania. Dating back to 1488, it was built by Stephen the Great, who repeatedly thwarted Ottoman forces trying to move west into the region. The story goes that it was built as a thank-you to a local monk who offered Stephen advice before one of his many battles.

"It is almost impossible to describe the impact of the paintings on the outside walls of the church when you first behold them," Bay says. "The power of the colors so boldly splashed across the surface is what first assaults the eye, as though the building has been transformed into a spiritual stone canvas. Mixed in with that cornucopia of colors is a swirling riot of visual images—celestial ladders, whole arrays of saints, hell and heaven in all their glory and fury. It's almost deranged, most certainly psychedelic, a canvas expressing the entirety of the Christian story, all slapped onto low-slung stone walls topped by an incongruous roof.

"As your eye begins to decipher the imagery and your quickened heart calms down to interpret the stories that are being told, the anarchy of your first impressions gives way to a reasoned understanding of this hauntingly beautiful, ethereal picture book. On entering the churches, the seeming psychedelia is replaced by a sonorous solemnity, as the imposing presence of the elders of the church, saints, founders, and patrons cover every available square inch of the interior, asserting the theological lineage and justification of the monastery and its role as spiritual mentor to the soul's journey."

40

SIPPING IN SOUTH AFRICA

WHY: Stunning scenery and a burgeoning wine culture make South Africa
a premium destination for oenophiles.

W HEN I WENT TO SOUTH AFRICA IN 1995 to scout its potential as a wine-touring destination, I didn't think it was ready," Patricia Nicholls, who creates XO Travel Consultant's exclusive wine and gastronomy tours, says. "Though there had been some incredible successes, like the Kanonkop Pinotage, the industry was more quantity than quality, and many vintners couldn't find a market for their wines outside of the country. Since that time, there's been an enormous change. Today you find many vintages from the Winelands region showing up on Top 100 lists and winning gold medals; additionally, there are many smaller family wineries making perfect wines but not selling them internationally. When you combine a wine exploration with some cultural sightseeing—and since you're in South Africa, a visit to a game park— you have a winning formula. I've led a number of groups to South Africa who've done many wine-tasting trips around the world, and they always say that this is their favorite."

South Africa's preeminent wine-growing region, the Winelands, is a short distance from the city of Cape Town, and analogies with Napa Valley and San Francisco are common—and well founded. Like San Francisco, Cape Town is both cosmopolitan and manageable, a cityscape with a Mediterranean climate that's well ensconced in its natural surroundings. Like Napa and Sonoma valleys, the vineyards of the Winelands are set in a series of picturesque valleys between low mountains and can be reached on day trips or enjoyed from posh resorts nearby. Nicholls builds her tasting tours around not only the most prominent wineries but those that revel in opening their doors and minds to visitors. "We visit winemakers who are willing to be probed," she says. "It's not just sipping and spitting. We sample the latest and greatest, and get an understanding of what the winemakers are thinking and where they're going."

XO Travel Consultants' South African wine adventure is divided into three segments—Cape

Rovos Rail, whose suites are considered the best railroad berths in the world, spirits oenophiles north to South Africa's famed game parks.

Town and the Winelands region; a voyage north on Rovos Rail; and a stay at a safari lodge in the Sabi Sand Game Reserve. During the first leg of the trip, you'll generally split time between the Mount Nelson Hotel in Cape Town and the Grande Roche in the Winelands. "The Nellie," as the Mount Nelson is affectionately known, is set at the base of majestic Table Mountain, among sprawling gardens that provide an oasis near the heart of Cape Town's city center. Rooms look out on the Nellie's gardens, the pool, or the mountain. The Grande Roche rests in the Draken-stein Valley at the heart of the Winelands, on the site of a plantation dating back to 1717. Peren-nially ranked among the world's best country hotels, the Grande Roche boasts Africa's only Relais Gourmand restaurant, Bosman's.

The wineries Nicholls leads guests to will vary depending on the year's vintages, but several that are almost certain to be on the list include Klein Constantia, Meerlust Estate, and Thelema. Klein Constantia is a major producer of Vin de Constantia, a sweet white wine first produced here in the late 1600s. Meerlust is one of South Africa's most venerable wineries, established by the Myburgh family in 1756. They've built a modern reputation around their Pinotage, perhaps South Africa's most celebrated varietal. Thelema Mountain Vineyards occupies the site of a former fruit orchard on the slopes of Simonsberg Mountain. A veritable baby next to Meerlust and Klein Constantia (its land was given over to wine production in 1983), Thelema is best known for its Chardonnay and Cabernet.

During the Cape Town portion of the trip, Nicholls loves to expose you to at least one meal of authentic Cape Dutch cuisine. "It's really an offshoot of Malaysian food, a result of the cook-ing of the Indonesian slaves that the Dutch brought here in the seventeenth century," she says. "There are curries (*potjies* in Afrikaaner) and *bobotie,* a delicately spiced beef stew. Locals also love their barbecues or *braais,* which consist of fish or farm-raised game meat like springbok, kudu, or ostrich."

Most of South Africa's famed game parks are in the Mpumalanga Province, at the opposite end of the country from Cape Town. There's no more stylish way to travel the 1,000 miles north to the gateway city of Pretoria than in one of the thirty-six elegantly appointed suites of the Rovos Rail. "Some of my clients are surprised (and perhaps dismayed) when they learn that we're going to be on a train for two days," Nicholls says. "But they come away impressed." The handsome wood-paneled suites on Rovos are the largest and best appointed in the world, with en suite bathrooms with shower. (A Royal Suite, which takes up half a carriage, is 170 square feet, and features a Victorian-style tub.) Nicholls makes sure that the dining room is stocked with more wines of interest, so you can continue your South African viticultural education as you roll north. The train follows the Old Karoo Pioneering Trail and showcases a microcosm of

South Africa's shifting landscapes—from the mountain ranges in the south to the barren deserts of the Great Karoo to the grasslands of the Highveld.

From Pretoria, you'll take a motorcoach to a safari lodge. One favorite is MalaMala, which looks out on the Sand River. There are three different accommodations at MalaMala—the main lodge, the Sable Camp, and Rattray's. All offer air-conditioned bars and libraries, expansive wildlife-viewing decks, and rooms with "his/her" bathrooms. The *khayas* (Zulu for "home") at Rattray's evoke the Africa of Hemingway's heyday, with leather sofas, crystal, and the added touches of a private garden and plunge pool.

Game drives out of MalaMala are led in the Sabi Sand Game Reserve. "Much of Kruger National Park has been macadammed over," Nicholls offers, "and there are places where you feel like you're in the middle of Piccadilly Circus. MalaMala uses dirt tracks and is overall smaller than the big lodges operating in Kruger. You feel like you're on your own." Game-viewing safaris (by jeep) are conducted in the early morning and late afternoon. Sabi Sand is one of the best places in South Africa to spot leopards and lions; hyenas, elephants, rhinos, hippos, and giraffes are also regularly encountered.

"On the last night of our trip, there's a special surprise," Nicholls says. "As people are enjoying sundowners, we gather everyone up and load into the jeeps. We go through the dark a bit, and then this lit-up area comes into view. When you get closer, you realize it's a candlelight dinner, all set up in the middle of the veldt. The meal could be grilled springbok or karoo lamb, served with a complement of top-notch South African wines. Everything tastes better under the stars."

41

THE FAIRY CHIMNEYS OF CAPPADOCIA

WHY: The sandstone formations, hillside structures, and underground cities of
Cappadocia are utterly surreal and add an exciting dimension to Turkish travel.

W ITH THE BLACK CLOUD OF THE MOVIE *MIDNIGHT EXPRESS* decades in the past,
Turkey has emerged as an invigorating travel destination. There's Istanbul, metaphorically straddling Europe and Asia over the Bosporus Strait, with its clash of old and new and its approachable exoticism. There's the Turquoise Coast from Antalya to Bodrum along the Mediterranean, with its mix of sunken archaeological ruins and lonely sheltered bays that have been beckoning yachters away from the better-known Greek Isles.

And there's another destination in Turkey that's a bit off the beaten path but that has captivated travelers who've made the trip: the region of Cappadocia. Situated near the center of Turkey, southwest of the city of Kayseri, Cappadocia is close to the volcanoes of Hasan and Erciyes, which are responsible for its otherworldly appeal. Eruptions at least three million years ago formed a tableland of sedimentary rocks, and tens of thousands of years of wind, rain, and floods from the Kizilirmak River eroded the soft stone to create a bizarre, undulating rock landscape, with conical formations that are reminiscent of minarets. Most striking among these are the fairy chimneys (or fairy towers), pinnacles that stand as tall as 130 feet, with caps of rock balanced on the top. Beneath a thin exterior of basalt, the lava rock in these formations was soft enough to be carved by inhabitants to create homes, churches, and even underground cities. (Paranormal expert Andrew Collins has written that local lore referred to them as *peri bacalari,* or the fire chimneys of the Peri, a group of fallen angels associated with Iblis, the Arab-Persian form of Satan. Somewhere along the way, *fire* became *fairy.*)

As you're driving from the airport at Kayseri to the town of Göreme, the fairy chimneys dotting the landscape let you know that you've arrived at someplace quite different. This is confirmed when you reach your hotel—a cave hotel. One such property, Anatolian Houses, occupies five attached cave formations that were once used as dwellings and places of worship by Cap-

A hot-air balloon ride over Cappadocia provides a perfect perspective to take in the otherworldly landscape of fairy chimneys.

padocia's early Christian residents, circa A.D. 200. (Most of the cave dwellings have been vacant for hundreds of years, though there's a trend toward conversion of caves into second homes and boutique hotels; other cave hotels include Serinn and Cappadocia Cave Suites.) This is not camping but a luxury hotel. Being in the rock, not attached to or on top of it, the rooms stay cool during the day and can be chilly at night, though there's a fireplace to keep you comfortable (as well as central heating, LCD television, and a heated indoor/outdoor pool).

"One of my finest dinners in Turkey was at Anatolian Houses," *Travel + Leisure* A-list travel consultant Anne Scully recalls. "From our table on the terrace, we looked out over the valley, with other cave dwellings and fairy towers in the foreground and the sun setting behind. The food throughout the region is Mediterranean—luscious yogurt (nothing like you have at home), fresh apricots, flat breads grilled on the fire,

"I've never been anywhere where the landscape so begged to be floated over."

kebabs of lamb and chicken, grilled vegetables, all strongly spiced and very flavorful. And not overly filling." After dinner—or before, for that matter—you can help yourself to a glass of cheer from the wine fountain that flows in the hotel's courtyard. Though Turkey's largely Islamic population refrains from alcohol, the wine industry here goes back six thousand years, and the country has fifty wineries; the Cappadocia region is a major producer.

One could easily wander the valleys of Cappadocia for days, discovering nearly hidden dwellings and humble chapels scraped from the soft volcanic rock by the early Christians. The greatest concentration of these structures is on display at the Göreme Open-Air Museum, essentially a largely intact carved village, including a number of small churches. Some of the churches, which date back to the eleventh century, have wonderful frescoes. The Dark Church, so named because there's but one small window allowing light to penetrate, has especially well-preserved paintings of New Testament scenes. Nearby is the Girls' Tower, a six-story convent carved in the rocks that's believed to have housed up to three hundred nuns at a time.

To evade persecutors—first the Romans and later invading Arabs—the early Christians of Cappadocia went underground . . . literally. Whole subterranean villages were constructed, with tunnels connecting natural caves and carved spaces; some of the villages extend down as far as a quarter of a mile. (Archaeologists, citing scrapings made by rock tools as opposed to the metal tools in use by early Christians, believe that some of the villages were carved as early as 1,200 B.C. by Hittite peoples. Residents did not live underground full-time but retreated to their below-ground lairs when enemies were spotted in the vicinity.) Squeezing through discreet entries once obscured by stone doors that could be rolled in and out of place at Kaymakli (one of the villages that can be toured), you'll enter a self-contained world of air and waste shafts and connecting passageways. Kaymakli has four levels: the lower level housed livestock pens and a small church; the second, another church and living spaces; the third, wine/olive oil presses and kitchens with hearths for cooking (chimneys were vented to the exterior); and the fourth, storage space. Many of the walls are charred black from the burning of innumerable torches. The ingenuity of the ventilation systems and the longevity of these structures, given the soft stone and their long history, both give pause.

If you visit Cappadocia, one must-do experience is a balloon trip over the valleys of the fairy chimneys. "I've never been anywhere where the landscape so begged to be floated over," Scully says. "It was akin to floating above the moon." A ballooning morning at Cappadocia begins early, as you won't want to miss the rising sun playing off the spires. After coffee and a pastry to tide you over until a proper breakfast, you'll be driven to the ballooning site. Here, a number of balloons, each fashioned from multicolored squares of silk, are spread out on the ground; guests are often taken aback at their large size. As the fires are stoked, the balloons slowly come alive, building your anticipation as you watch your vehicle take shape. The balloon is held down by weights, and once guests have climbed into the basket ("It's very easy; I saw octogenarians and people in wheelchairs get in," Scully says), the weights are released. The balloon lifts very softly; there's no thrust of an engine, and one can nearly hear a collective "ooh" and "aah" from assembled passengers. The pilot controls the height of the craft by monitoring the amount of hot air that's released into the balloon. As the sun rises, the pinnacles and valley walls take on brilliant hues of ochre, umber, pink, and lavender, and the crisp outside air begins to warm. The apricots that grow in such great abundance here shine orange. If winds are cooperative, your pilot will be able to drop you down just above a tree so you can pick a sun-warmed apricot, a prebreakfast treat, as the wicker basket brushes the treetops. The balloon can be controlled with such precision that it can hover close enough to the fairy chimneys for you to observe the holes where pigeons dwell.

When your balloon sets down, you can celebrate your good fortune with a toast of champagne and cherry juice. "Floating above the treetops in the open air of a balloon, you feel like you're a bird," Scully reminisces. "Between flying in the balloon, scrambling around on the ladders of the cave hotel, and exploring the underground villages, you feel like a child again. Cappadocia does something to help you live in the moment."

IN THE CITY

TRAVELERS SEEKING STIMULATION AND CULTURAL REVIVAL WILL OFTEN FLOCK TO A CITY, AND THE URBAN-ORIENTED ADVENTURES IN this section take you from Paris to Jaipur to Hanoi and mix fine cuisine, five-star accommodation, and artistic milestones along the way.

For opera buffs, there's "The World's Greatest Opera Houses," which spirits you by private jet to take in some of the Continent's most extraordinary houses; it includes behind-the-scenes perquisites—like receiving a singing lesson from a Czech Opera ensemble member on the stage of Prague's Theatre of the Estates. In Rajasthan, you'll be intoxicated by a riot of colors and the very energy of the country—and meet some of the finest miniaturist painters and jewelry makers. In Vietnam, you'll move from Dalat to Hanoi, walking through city neighborhoods and the adjoining countryside where you'll be overwhelmed by the warmth of the nation's people and their remarkable culinary prowess. Riding the *Orient-Express* from Paris to Istanbul, you'll couple the sophisticated panache of the world's most-famous train with a sweeping journey across Europe.

The Burj Al Arab defines Dubai's skyline and is one of the world's most distinctive hotels.

42

Tea, Tango, and Malbec:
From Buenos Aires to Mendoza

WHY: The sophistication and excitement of Argentina's leading cities come to
life as you dance and taste your way from the pampas to the Andes.

FROM THE WINDSWEPT HILLS OF TIERRA DEL FUEGO at the southern end of the
continent to the glaciers of Patagonia to the fertile pampas region surrounding Buenos
Aires, Argentina is both vast and dizzyingly varied. Voyagers could hardly hope to experience
the country's diverse landscapes and cultures in one pass-through. But city lovers can get a tantalizing taste of urban Argentina with a whirlwind visit to Buenos Aires and Mendoza.

European influence—particularly Spanish and Italian—is especially strong in Buenos Aires,
the nation's capital city and arguably the most influential cultural and business center in South
America. "If you took Manhattan and spread it out, added attractive old buildings and beautiful
parks with mature trees, and sprinkled the whole package with a Continental flavor, you'd have
Buenos Aires," South America and Asia luxury-travel consultant Brooke Garnett observes.

Your base in Buenos Aires is the Palacio Duhau Park Hyatt. Situated on Avenida Alvear, Buenos Aires's most fashionable street, the Park Hyatt is actually two structures: the historic palace
and a newer structure, separated by classical gardens and connected by a series of art and sculp-
ture galleries below the gardens. You enter through the original structure, where a lobby of
chandeliers and marble harkens to the palace's past, and the glass-encased wine cellar in the
adjacent lounge speaks to the future. The Park Hyatt's rooms combine dark wood fixtures and
comforting earth tones with modern touches like flat-screen televisions, bedside curtain controls, and walk-in rain showers.

Your first day in Buenos Aires you'll have a chance to take in some of the city's landmarks,
including La Recoleta Cemetery, resting place of Evita Perón. On day two you'll have several
special appointments. The first will be high tea with Ines Berton, whose acute sense of taste

Much of the produce served at Cavas Wine Lodge is grown in the lodge's gardens.

and smell have helped her become one of the world's foremost tea experts. She'll meet you at L'Orangerie, one of the restaurants in the venerable Alvear Palace Hotel. Here, overlooking Jardin d'Hiver (one of Argentina's most elegant formal gardens), white-gloved waiters serve mini patisserie and fresh-fruit tartlets as Berton steeps and pours some of her favorite teas—perhaps Darjeeling Imperial, Ceylon Pettiapalla, or Jasmine Flowers. "Ines's teas not only taste wonderful, they look beautiful," Garnett says, "almost like potpourri." After the initial tasting, Berton will inquire about your flavor preferences and create a custom blend just for you, working from a collection of teas she's carried along in small tin cans."

"I can't imagine anyone who's at all interested in dance coming away from Rojo Tango feeling anything but enthralled."

The teas blended and served by Ines Berton may have a calming effect on your person, but don't get too relaxed—your private tango lesson awaits. The tango was born around 1880 in the brothels of Buenos Aires. The music mixed gaucho verse with Spanish and Italian melodies brought west by new immigrants; the dance moves developed to, uh, foster closer interaction between guests and employees. Your venue will be the hip Faena Hotel & Universe, with its mirrored tables, benches upholstered in black pony hair, and gold-leafed chairs. Your instructors are members of the celebrated Rojo Tango ensemble that performs regularly in the Faena Tango Salon. "There are eight steps you need to learn to perform the basic tango," Garnett explains. "The rest of the tango is improvisational, with the woman following her partner's lead."

There's time for a cocktail before you adjourn to the Faena Tango Salon, with its deep red velvet upholstered chairs and shimmering silver place settings. Here you'll settle in for a fine dinner of Argentinian steak or salmon complemented by local wine or champagne. As your dishes are cleared, the Rojo Tango ensemble emerges from all corners of the room, and the show begins around the diners. "There are twenty to twenty-five performers between dancers and musicians," Garnett says. "The musicians come out in white suits with spotlights illuminating them. The women are clad in very sexy dresses; one buxom vocalist's dress seemed to stay on only with the help of safety pins. You will quickly recognize your instructor from the lesson before dinner." There are many costume changes and many dances, each telling a small story. The tangos become more frenetic and acrobatic as the show progresses. "Some visitors to Buenos Aires end up at one of the larger tango shows and come away a bit disappointed," Garnett adds. "I can't imagine anyone who's at all interested in dance or show business coming away from Rojo Tango feeling anything but enthralled." Your instructor will be waiting after the show to spirit you away to a local *milonga* (tango salon) where you can practice some new moves. Nightlife in Buenos Aires goes *all night;* clubgoers leaving at the first light of dawn are likely to find new dancers waiting in line to get in.

The next morning, you'll leave Buenos Aires for the Andean city of Mendoza. Wherever you look from the city's wide, tree-lined streets, snowcapped peaks are in sight. "Mendoza has much of the appeal of Buenos Aires," Garnett says, "though it's smaller and more quaint. It also has a European feel, with several large squares and many cafés where you can enjoy a cappuccino and people watch."

Mendoza's sunny climate, abundance of water (from rivers flowing out of the Andes), and mineral-rich soil have combined to make this Argentina's primary wine-growing region. Many don't realize that Argentina is the fifth-largest wine producer in the world; some 75 percent of its vintages come from Mendoza, with the area's Malbec enjoying a growing international reputation. You'll spend most of your time in Mendoza in the heart of the winelands—the Lujan de Cuyo district—at the exquisite Cavas Wine Lodge. The lodge rests in the center of a 35-acre vineyard of Bonada grapes, a light red varietal introduced from Italy's Piedmont region. Accommodations at this Relais & Châteaux property are in one of fourteen freestanding adobe villas. Each Mediterranean-inspired bungalow has an interior courtyard with a bubbling fountain, a private plunge pool, fireplaces, and a minimalist decor that accentuate the beauty of the Andes and the vineyards; you can take in the views from your private deck as you enjoy a picnic of Serrano ham and arugula sandwiches and local cheeses.

Cavas is a perfect base for wine tasting in Lujan de Cuyo, and the property's concierge can arrange private tours of some of the leading wineries, including major producers like Catena Zapata and Achaval Ferrer, as well as boutique operations like Carlos Pulenta. Some twenty-five wineries are nearby. The viticultural focus here, as elsewhere in Mendoza, is on Malbecs, which were introduced to Argentina from France in the nineteenth century; these spirited reds are characterized by an inky blackish-purple color and prominent plum aroma. You can also avail yourself of the lodge's impeccable cellar, which holds 250 Mendoza wines, including the Bonarda that's cultivated on the property. Should you wish, a private dinner can be arranged in the cellar, or you can enjoy a tasting tour of Mendoza in the Cavas dining room.

Any lingering aches from your exploits in the *milongas* of Buenos Aires can be chased away in the Cavas spa, where a menu of "vinotherapy" treatments—including a Malbec-seed body wrap—await. Malbec, it seems, is everywhere in Mendoza. Relax and drink it in.

43

ISTANBUL BY *ORIENT-EXPRESS*

WHY: Experience the glamour and allure of riding the world's most famous
train as it courses along the latitudes of Europe.

THERE ARE FASTER WAYS TO GET FROM PARIS TO ISTANBUL. There are certainly more frugal ways. But you'll be hard-pressed to find a more elegant, romantic, unforgettable manner of conveyance than the *Venice Simplon-Orient-Express*. "People come to ride on the *Orient-Express* to relive the glamour of its most famous years—the period between World War I and World War II," the train's manager Bruno Janssens explains, "a period that conjures the characters of Agatha Christie, of spies, royalty, and intrigue. Looking back, it's difficult to say where history ends and Christie's fictional world begins, but I've often thought that much of Europe's fortunes in that tumultuous period were determined on the train."

On its six-day/five-night passage from Paris to Istanbul, the *VSOE* traverses the heart of continental Europe, running through sections of eight countries—France, Switzerland, Lichtenstein, Germany, Austria, Hungary, Romania, and Bulgaria—before reaching Turkey. Coursing through fertile river lands, steep mountains, and broad plains, it offers an excursion into the glories of travel on the world's most famous train and a sweeping glimpse of current-day Europe.

Since the train's inaugural run in 1883, the phrase *Orient-Express* has meant different things at different times. The first route, which ran from Paris to Giurgiu, Romania, via Munich and Vienna, was made possible in part by the introduction of the first railroad restaurant car by a Belgian railway enthusiast named Georges Nagelmackers; he essentially did for train cuisine what George Pullman did a few decades before for train sleeping. By 1889, the train was making it all the way to Istanbul. While other trains ran the route from France to Turkey, the train Christie readers know began running as the *Simplon-Orient-Express* in 1921. The turmoil of World War II and its negative economic aftermath sounded the death knell for the famed train;

OPPOSITE *Chefs take on supplies. Despite a tiny kitchen area, the* Venice Simplon-Orient-Express *creates food on par with Michelin-star restaurants.* FOLLOWING PAGES Orient-Express *passengers dine in each of the three dining cars—the Etoile du Nord (shown here), the Chinoise, and the Lalique.*

the opulence of its golden era faded and faded until service ceased altogether in 1977. Later that year, the *Orient-Express*'s resuscitation began when entrepreneur James B. Sherwood bought two of the train's carriages at auction. He went on to acquire and restore other stately cars from Europe's golden age of railways, and by 1982, regular service had returned between London and Venice. The Istanbul route was reinstated in 1999.

"The interiors of the cars have been re-created to emulate the environs of the late 1920s," Janssens says. "In keeping with this spirit, there are no showers in the room; every other night of the journey we spend in a hotel, in part so guests can enjoy a bath or shower. While the train offers double cabins and suites, most guests bound for Istanbul opt for the two-room suites, which provide a sitting room and sleeping quarters. The atmosphere on board is quite formal. Jackets and ties are required at luncheon; guests wear formal attire at dinner. Again, this harkens back to earlier, more elegant times." One hundred guests board the fifteen-car *Venice Simplon-Orient-Express* midafternoon at the Paris Gare de l'Est station, where they are greeted by a cadre of staff and shepherded to their suite, for afternoon tea. Each sleeping car has a dedicated steward who is available twenty-four hours a day. He'll also serve you breakfast en suite after those nights that you're on the train.

As the train moves through the suburbs east of Paris, the modern, urban landscape begins to fall away. When the line joins the Seine and twilight begins to envelop the surrounding country-side, riders will change into their evening finery and assemble in the Bar Car, at the center of the train. "There's a pianist on hand, but I think much of the entertainment comes from guests discovering each other," Janssens says. "Guests may take dinner at their leisure in one of three dining cars—the Etoile du Nord, the Chinoise, or the Lalique. Each car has its own personality, and we make sure everyone has a chance to dine at least once in each car. I think my favorite is the Lalique, with its faint-blue glass moldings made by the famed glassmaker. Our chefs are French, and the cuisine reflects that. The quality is very close to that of a one-star Michelin restaurant, which is a small miracle considering how difficult conditions are in a miniature kitchen on a moving train."

Somewhere between Zurich and the Austrian border, most travelers will be swayed to sleep by the rhythm of the train. Sunrise will find the distinctive blue and gold cars of the *VSOE* somewhere near Salzburg. Early risers may be treated to the sight of the majestic Hohensalz-burg Castle straddling the hillside near the station. The peaks of the Salzkammergut region sparkle in the sun as a breakfast of fresh pastries, fruit salad, juice, and coffee or tea is served in your room. Soon afterward, the line joins the Danube, which it follows much of the morning. Lunchtime will find you around Vienna; from here it's not long until you reach the Hungarian border, where the engine is switched (it's customary for the *VSOE* to change engines at each border). "We reach Nyugati station in Budapest midafternoon, and there's a Hungarian band playing on the platform," Janssens explains. "There's actually a band in every station where we disembark; we do little things to make the trip very special, and since the train runs this route only once a year, local people along the route are genuinely excited to see it arrive. You'll spend this evening off the train at the elegant Sofitel Budapest Maria Dorottya on the banks of the Danube. You'll board the train the next afternoon to cross the Great Alföld plain en route to Romania."

Whenever possible, the *VSOE* attempts to replicate the route and stops of the original train. This includes disembarking on Monday morning at the Romanian town of Sinaia, in the Carpathian Mountains. Here you'll visit the Peleş Castle, a former summer palace of King Carol I (who liberated Romania) that was completed just in time to host the guests on the *VSOE*'s inaugural run. From Sinaia, it's just a few hours' ride to Bucharest, where you'll spend a second night off the train. Here, your accommodation will be the historic Athénée Palace Hilton Bucharest hotel, set in the heart of the city. Built in 1914, the Athénée was a stopping point for interwar *Orient-Express* travelers and, like the train, is associated with intrigue. The acoustics of the lobby are such that a person in the right spot can overhear conversations whispered in confidence at the other end of the room. It's been said that Gestapo agents believed that knowledge of this acoustical secret was theirs alone, and that certain journalists would delight in supplying them with misinformation.

You'll reboard the train the next morning, with one more full day on the *VSOE* and one of the most memorable moments on the train ahead—the crossing of the Danube at Giurgiu into Bulgaria. "Here the river is huge, three miles wide, and the bridge is high and squeaky," Janssens says. "The train goes very slowly, and the crossing underscores the sense that you are moving into a country that many travelers have not ever visited." After another engine change, the *VSOE* rolls toward the Black Sea and the ancient city of Varna, retracing the original 1883 route. After one last night lingering in the Bar Car or hovering over dessert in Lalique, you'll retire. When you awake, the spires of the Eastern Orthodox cathedrals of Eastern Europe will have given way to the minarets of Islamic mosques as you descend across the Thracian Plain.

"As we pull into Sirkeci Station, there's a local band playing very loudly," Janssens notes. "Some guests are crying as they prepare to leave us. I think they've felt that under our care, they had no worries in the world as they traveled the breadth of Europe."

44

The World's Greatest Opera Houses by Private Jet

WHY: What opera lover wouldn't swoon for a chance to visit Europe's greatest opera houses by private jet to take in rare performances with exclusive backstage access?

FOR OPERA BUFFS, THE CHANCE TO SEE A STAR SOPRANO at the Paris Opéra or the Mariinsky in Saint Petersburg is reason for applause. Imagine, then, the opportunity to attend nightly performances in Paris, Saint Petersburg, Prague, and Vienna—plus exclusive behind-the-scenes engagements, Michelin-star dining, and travel by private jet.

Bravo!

"My goal was to create a one-of-a-kind experience—an unforgettable odyssey of culture and exclusive access," says Jacqueline Porter, the impresaria behind the thirteen-day World's Greatest Opera Houses by Private Jet tour. Given the opulence of the trip's settings, even the tone-deaf will appreciate its extravagance, made possible by Porter's extensive connections in the arts world; she was a professional dancer and actress and later worked in fund-raising and development for symphony orchestras.

Paris is the first stop for you and a maximum of ten other guests on your Gulfstream 550, and you'll touch down in time to rest before donning formal wear for the Paris Opéra's May Gala. "The Paris Opéra is the most glamorous operatic body in Europe," Porter says. "La Scala and Vienna are very exciting, but there's only one Paris. The May Gala is the Paris Opéra's major fund-raiser, and all of Parisian society is there. One year, we were treated to Anna Netrebko playing Juliet in *The Capulets and the Montagues* by Bellini. Netrebko's been a superstar for years, but incredibly, this was her Paris Opéra debut!" After enjoying a glamorous diva's performance from orchestra seats, guests enjoy a VIP dinner at the opera house with donors and corporate sponsors. The room sparkles with the latest creations from Chanel, Celine, Dior, and Nina

You'll visit the Vienna Opera House on the fourth leg of your whirlwind tour of Europe's great opera houses.

Ricci and jewels by Boucheron, Cartier, Van Cleef & Arpels, and Chaumet. (Note: While programs and performers will vary from year to year, Porter assures her guests seats to each opera season's most prized performances and the world's finest classical stars.)

Before leaving Paris, guests are treated to another rare privilege—a private Chanel couturier appointment. The Chanel store will close its doors in the middle of the day, and you'll have the undivided attention of the staff, a bottomless glass of champagne, and privacy to tour the store with a personal shopper. "There's no pressure to make a purchase—but as you stand being fussed over in the Chanel mirrors, it's thrilling to think of the luminaries who've stood where you are, decades or even hours before you," Porter notes. The day ends with another performance—in 2008 it was Venezuelan wunderkind Gustavo Dudamel leading the Orchestre Philharmonique de Radio France at Salle Pleyel, with debonair violinist Nikolaj Znaider.

> "Throwing sounds out into the opera house where Mozart once conducted is a one-of-a-kind thrill."

After four nights in Paris, your jet flies across northern Europe, touching down on the shores of the Baltic in time for Saint Petersburg's White Nights Music Festival, a celebration of both Russian music and late spring. ("White Nights" references the almost constant daylight in Saint Petersburg at this time of year.) The event is coordinated by Maestro Valery Gergiev, the Russian musical giant who singlehandedly resuscitated the Mariinsky Opera and Ballet (formerly the Kirov). "He's often referred to as 'the busiest conductor on the planet,' but he is deeply engaged in the well-being and advancement of the Mariinsky and is present throughout the White Nights," Porter explains. "Guests get to meet him onstage after the performance."

Beyond the opera and ballet performances, your three-night stay in Saint Petersburg holds a number of surprises and exclusive Porter touches. There's a floating dinner on the city's famed canals, complete, of course, with good Russian caviar and champagne. There's private access to the venerable Hermitage museum, which houses 3 million pieces, from seventh-century Russian jewels to Picassos; your docent speaks fluent English. Most remarkable, guests will attend a private rehearsal of the Saint Petersburg Philharmonic—a privilege never before available to anyone but heads of state. Likewise, you'll attend a private class of the Mariinsky Ballet, another first for visitors. "We're there as spectators and are expected to watch quietly," Porter explains, "but if the dancers invite interaction, well, all the better!"

Soon it's farewell to Maestro Gergiev and welcome to Prague, where you'll spend three nights. After a brief respite in your deluxe Four Seasons room, you'll take to the Vltava for a boat ride and overview of the rich cultural history of this great Czech city. In the evening, you'll attend a performance at the Theatre of the Estates—the very house where Mozart premiered *Don Giovanni* in 1787. Pay close attention to the techniques of the players in the lead roles, as the following day you'll take the stage with a leading member of the Czech Opera for a master class. "Throwing sounds out into the opera house where Mozart once conducted is a one-of-a-kind thrill," Porter enthuses. "We'll learn the basics of opera singing, and our patient instructor will coach us through perfect delivery of a line from a Mozart aria. Your friends at home will be awestruck when you toss off a snippet from *The Marriage of Figaro* or *The Magic Flute*." Guests also attend performances in the country's crown jewels: the National Theatre of Prague and the Prague State Opera.

No whirlwind tour of northern Europe's great opera houses would be complete without a visit to Vienna and the Vienna State Opera. Here, you'll have royal box seating for the current performance; a recent season's production featured Renée Fleming. On the morning of your departure, there's the option of attending a mass in the Hapsburg Chapel, which includes a performance of the Vienna Boys' Choir. Before lunch, it's royal box seating for another Vienna "must"—the Lipizzaner stallions. The Lipizzaner breed was developed by the Hapsburg nobility in the late sixteenth century and has been trained ever since in a highly specialized tradition at Vienna's Spanish Riding School. The stallions are educated in the haute ecole movements of classical dressage, showcased in their performance at the spectacular Winter Riding School in the Imperial Palace. "The Lipizzaners are athletic, graceful, awesome!" Porter exclaims. "They're impeccable artists, both horses and trainers. Seeing them perform on their elegant native turf is a lifetime must. My guests will be among the first in four hundred thirty years to meet the stallions afterward."

45

INTRO TO INDIA: RAJASTHAN

WHY: Experience India at its colorful, mystical best, without a grueling
itinerary or the rigors of the megacities.

A S A FORMER EDITOR OF A TRAVEL MAGAZINE, I'd been just about everywhere and had been trying to visit India for twenty years," *Town & Country* editor in chief Pamela Fiori recalls. "I'd plan trips and then end up postponing them, for one reason or another. India was too big, too poor, too complicated, too unstable. A point in time came when I realized that I didn't have to try and see all of India in one sweeping trip. I could choose a part of India that seemed doable for someone who had not been there before and consider a visit to this region as an introduction.

"Rajasthan was the obvious choice. It proved to be a perfect way to ease into India. Rajasthan has some of the most beautiful little cities and a mix of terrains—both farmland and desert. What I didn't expect was the majesty of the place, and the incredible colors. The women were regal in even the poorest villages, adorned with lovely colorful saris, long earrings, bangles up their arms, and necklaces. Whether they were real gems or fake, they looked fantastic, even glamorous. The poverty most westerners associate with India is there, but it's not so desperate as to make your head spin. You never become inured to it, but you can accept the reality of it, and most of the people I saw had retained their dignity."

Rajasthan, situated in India's northwest corner, adjacent to Pakistan, is the country's largest state, encompassing over 130,000 square miles. Much of the region west of the Aravalli Range is given over to the Thar Desert; east of the mountains, the land is more hospitable to agricultural efforts. In the spirit of maintaining a pace leisurely enough to get a feel for the place, Fiori recommends visiting three of Rajasthan's most colorful cities: Udaipur in the south, Jodhpur in the west, and Jaipur in the northeast.

"Udaipur, set on Pichola Lake, is a stunningly beautiful city," Fiori says. "My memories of the city are marked by two very different moods—the languorous disposition of the Taj Lake Palace

OPPOSITE *Exterior walls in the city of Jodhpur are painted blue to refract heat and ward off mosquitoes.* FOLLOWING PAGES *The Amber Fort, one of the visitor attractions in Jaipur, is best reached by elephant.*

hotel and the frenetic feeling of the Udaipur bazaar." The Lake Palace, on 4-acre Jag Niwas Island, started life as the real pleasure palace of Prince Jagat Singh II in 1746. Today its opulent suites are decorated with silks, vivid murals, and ornately carved wood furniture. "At night, the lights of the city palace complex sparkle from across the lake," Fiori says, "and Indian music can be heard. It doesn't seem quite real. The bazaar, on the other hand, verges on being out of control but is fascinating. Elephants, camels, pigs, and cows jockey for position, as auto rickshaws snake their way among pedestrians. Each section showcases specific products—spices, shoes, housewares, and so on. Experiencing an Indian market is hair-raising, confusing, and thrilling, not to be attempted without a guide, but not to be missed."

A highlight of Udaipur from a crafts standpoint are the miniatures, small detailed paintings depicting Indian lore, with all the figures in profile. Though miniatures are rendered throughout Rajasthan, the art was developed in Udaipur at the Mewar school in the fifteenth century. At the Mayur Arts gallery, new miniatures are created and old ones sold, and you can observe painters at work with brushes made of a single hair of a squirrel. It's a treat to watch a work being created, and you can extend the pleasure by purchasing one to take home.

"I joked later to my New York friends that after a visit to India, you'll never wear black again."

There were sections of Fiori's trip where it made better sense—given her finite timetable—to take a private charter flight. But to reach her next stop, Jodhpur (Rajasthan's second-largest city), she and her husband, Colt Givner, chose to travel by car. While the roads of India can be rife with misfortune, her driver was up to the task. "He kept saying to us, as if a mantra, 'You need three things in India for a road trip: good luck, good horn, good brakes,' " Fiori says. "He was right, but traveling the roads gave us a sight of the India that many visitors miss. Each community could have provided the setting for an epic novel. Though the land was often a parched brown, the bright clothing of the villagers—especially the barefoot women—was a startling counterpoint. I joked later to my New York friends that after a visit to India, you'll never wear black again."

Jodhpur is called the Blue City, as many of its houses were painted that color by the Brahmans to cool them down in the summer heat and ward off mosquitoes. (The pants that bear the city's name were invented here by a polo-playing maharajah.) "Walking through the markets, I was taken with the unapologetic sensuality of the place," Fiori recalls, "the textures, from tie-dyed cottons to pashminas; the riot of colors, none of them subtle; and the jewels—rubies, emeralds, and sapphires in profusion. Perhaps this sensuality is why Western women I know have tended to respond much more enthusiastically to India than men."

Jaipur, Rajasthan's largest city, is called the Pink City for the shade of the plaster used in the old walled part of town. As Udaipur is known for its miniatures, Jaipur is known for its jewelry; it is home of the legendary Gem Palace, owned by the Kasliwal family, whom maharajahs from all over India (and other royals from around the world) have commissioned to create master-pieces since 1852. "There's a private not-for-sale collection of maharajahs' jewels that can be viewed by making an advance request with Sanjay Kasliwal, one of the palace's owners," Fiori says. "There are also strands of rubies and emeralds, and rings and earrings encrusted with pre-cious stones, that are for sale. For anyone even mildly interested in jewelry, it's a playground. I had to practically be pulled away by hand but still came away with enough jewelry to warrant buying a small safe." The Gem Palace is not the place to find deep discounts, but the quality of both the gems and the craftsmanship is impeccable.

One of the experiences Fiori looked forward to before her trip to India was the chance to ride on an elephant. She got that chance in Jaipur. "It turned out that elephant-back is the only practical way to get to the Amber Fort, a structure outside of town notable for its intricate carv-ings," she explains. "What's it like to ride on an elephant? Except for an occasional glimpse of your animal's ears, a bit of rocking and rolling, and the sight of elephants in front of you or pass-ing, you could be on a horse or in a vehicle. It's impossible to take a picture to prove it, so ask your guide to click the shutter for you."

46

MAGIC-CARPET RIDE IN IRAN

WHY: Iran boasts a warm and hospitable culture and a tradition of arts
excellence that's reflected in its brilliant carpets.

WHEN PEOPLE THINK OF IRAN," SAYS LUXURY-TRAVEL EXPERT Ken Fish, "they picture masses of chador-clad women waving their fists at the TV cameras, or kidnappings or the bluster of political figures. The reality on the ground could not be more different. Iran has one of the warmest, most hospitable cultures I've ever experienced. On a recent trip, our driver's parting words were 'Tell people in America we don't like them—we love them!'"

In Iran it seems that everyone is a poet. People have a deep level of introspection and a pride in Persia's long history. These facets of the nation have created a rich culture where the arts flourish. Perhaps Iran's most visible artistic achievement is its carpets. Carpet weaving is believed to go back at least 2,500 years. You can have an in-depth experience with this art form both by seeing antique carpets and by visiting modern-day carpet weavers.

In Tehran, you'll begin your education at the Carpet Museum of Iran, which exhibits a spectrum of carpets from all around the country. You'll also visit the private carpet museum of the late Rassam Arabzadeh, where thirty works of Iran's preeminent modern master weaver are displayed. The level of detail in Arabzadeh's work is astounding; carpets showing a peasant girl (*Qajar Girl*) and a scene in a royal court (*Cyrus the Great Ascends the Throne*) easily approach the intricacy of an oil painting. You'll also tour the city's largest carpet bazaar, an economic engine unto itself. As commentator Mustafa El-Labbad noted in the Egyptian weekly *Al-Ahram*: "The 'interests of the bazaar' comprise much more than livelihoods of the merchant and his supplier: they encompass the homes of the weavers, the workshops of the craftsmen who make the looms and other equipment and pervade deep into the countryside, where the sheep graze and the wool is shorn."

In Iran, carpets, more than anything else, have represented wealth. They gain value over time and are passed from generation to generation, with the finish of the pile improving with wear.

Carpet merchants like this gentleman are best approached in the company of someone who has the respect of the merchant.

Underscoring the carpets' significance is the fact that when people left Iran after the 1979 revolution, it was their carpets that they carried with them. Much of the work at the loom is done by women, who might make a million knots to create a square yard of premium-quality carpet.

"Part of our arrangement when we visit a town is that we connect with one of the local carpet experts," Fish explains. "When you go into the bazaar, it's better to enter with someone who has the respect of the merchants. This conveys respect to you. You'll work to develop a relationship with the merchant, often speaking through interpreters. It's important to be serious and respectful, to not impose yourself." There are many qualities by which the value of a carpet is assessed: the quality of the wool or silk, the quality of the dyes, and the number of knots per square foot (the more knots, the more prized the carpet), and, of course, whether the colors and pattern are pleasing to your eye. Your accompanying expert can help you identify carpets with the fewest imperfections and help you negotiate the deal.

Ken Fish has struck up friendships with carpet experts in some of the smaller cities, like Naein and Kashan. During these stops the local expert will take you to a workshop or even a family loom to see firsthand how the carpets are made. It's extremely painstaking work; weavers first attach vertical threads (the warp) to the loom's upper and lower beams. Horizontal threads (the weft) are interwoven with the warps to create a richly textured pile. After each line is knotted horizontally, threads are woven between alternating warps across the rug. The carpet's design is achieved through meticulous alternation of color; each tiny strand of wool or silk is individually knotted to the carpet's base.

Your tour of Iran will include highlights beyond your carpet adventures. The food is wonderful; lamb or mutton will take center stage at many meals, with accoutrements of dill-seasoned rice, hot nan, bean stews, pistachios, and dates rounding out the offering, and yogurt drinks to wash everything down. For many, the city of Isfahan in central Iran is a favorite, for its beautiful architecture, river views, and ample gardens that blossomed during the reign of the Safavids (a Shia dynasty that reunited Iran, ruling from 1501 to 1722). Among its many landmarks—including Imam Square, the world's second-largest public square—is the Abbasi Hotel, your home for three nights. Widely considered Iran's finest hotel, the Abbasi is on the grounds of a former caravanserai, bazaar, and school, and dates back to the seventeenth century. Its expansive courtyard—featuring a fine example of a Persian garden, alternating reflecting pools with greenery—is a place where guests can dine, sip tea, and relax under the stars.

A top quality 7-by-10-foot carpet may have 10,000,000 knots or more, each hand done.

47

A Night at the Burj Al Arab in Dubai

WHY: For lovers of unbridled luxury, Dubai—and the Burj Al Arab—
sets a seven-star standard.

D UBAI HAS ONE OF THE WORLD'S FASTEST-GROWING SKYLINES and is situated in the United Arab Emirates, one of the world's wealthiest countries. Given the city's zest for over-the-top architecture, its bustling commercial trade, and its burgeoning tourist appeal, it seems fitting that Dubai is home to one of humankind's most opulent, extravagant, and to some minds, slightly outrageous hotels—the Burj Al Arab.

The Burj Al Arab rises 1,053 feet above the Persian Gulf, where it rests 919 feet off Jumeirah Beach, on a manmade island constructed to serve as its foundation. The hotel is certainly Dubai's most distinctive building. It was designed by British architect Tom Wright to mimic the billowing sail of a dhow, the traditional Arab sailboat that plies the gulf below.

"When you make your reservations, the staff notes the exact time of your arrival," says celebrated food writer and cookbook author Monica Bhide. "A white Rolls-Royce is sent to the airport to fetch you. As you enter the Burj, they have staff flanking both sides of the entrance, waiting to gently spray you with rose water, a gesture of welcome and goodwill. You are also offered what might very well be the best dates and Arabic coffee in the world. This is typical warm Arab hospitality." You're assigned your own private butler, who will, among other things, unpack your suitcases and help you navigate the hotel's extensive pillow menu so you can be assured of having the perfect bolster for your sleep. The butler also sets up a full Arabic breakfast for you each morning—consisting of hummus, *foul* (a fava-bean dish), *labneh* (yogurt spread with olive oil), Arabic white cheese, parsley and onion omelets, and tea—in your en suite dining room. "My six-year-old who was with us summed up the look and feel of the Burj the best," Bhide says: " 'Mama, this looks like Aladdin's Agrabah!' "

Guests at Burj Al Arab are not likely to feel constrained in any of the 202 suites that stretch over the hotel's 27 stories. The suites have every amenity. The bath products are from Hermès, except

The opulence that characterizes the Burj Al Arab extends to the pool.

for the aromatherapy bath oils, which are personally mixed by your butler. There's a private bar in addition to your dining room, and a complete office outfitted with laptop computer.

As difficult as it might be to tear yourself away from the Burj Al Arab, greater Dubai has its attractions. The structure of urban Dubai is distinctive, to say the least—the city's main artery is a long line of skyscrapers, exactly one deep. Among Dubai's more curious development projects are the Palm Islands, a manmade archipelago in the Persian Gulf that will one day hold luxury homes, retail establishments, and hotels. The Hydropolis, the world's first luxury underwater hotel is said to have been inspired by Jules Verne's *20,000 Leagues Under the Sea*.

"It's definitely worthwhile to make a trip out to one of the desert resorts," Bhide says. "Here you can watch a falconry demonstration, take a camel trek, or do some dune-bashing with a four-wheel-drive vehicle." Of course, the Burj Al Arab can discreetly arrange any and all of these activities, and order a Rolls to spirit you around the city.

"My six-year-old summed up the look and feel of the Burj the best: 'Mama, this looks like Aladdin's Agrabah!'"

Nothing is ordinary at the Burj, and the emphasis on experience extends to dinner. Among the hotel's eight options, Al Mahara, a seafood restaurant on the Burj's main floor, stands out. Guests reach Al Mahara by a three-minute mock submarine ride, symbolically spiriting you to the bottom of the gulf. The focal point of the dining room is a gigantic oval aquarium.

Given the pillow selection, the elaborately tiled and marble-columned bathroom with circular whirlpool, a glass-enclosed shower stall, and twin vanities, the richly brocaded bed canopies, the bold blues, golds, purples, and reds of the silk upholstered furniture, the floor-to-ceiling windows looking out on the gulf, the private butler, and the countless other amenities offered by Burj Al Arab, one cannot resist asking: How was the night's sleep?

"Divine," Bhide says. "Simply divine."

48

WALKING AND EATING IN VIETNAM

WHY: The warmth and friendliness of the Vietnamese people will inspire you
as you visit country villages and bustling cities, from south to north.

FOR MUCH OF THE PAST TWO THOUSAND YEARS the people of Vietnam have suffered at the hands of foreign oppressors. But against all odds, they have remained genial and welcoming. "There's an openness, a friendliness that I haven't experienced in other parts of Asia," Michele Harvey, an international walking-tour leader, says. "Visitors to Vietnam inevitably fall in love with the people, and that's the reason to go."

A walking tour of Vietnam explores much of this long, narrow nation, from Dalat in the southern highlands to the capital of Hanoi in the north. You'll fly and drive from region to region, with each day featuring a different walk. They are a gentle two to three hours on easy terrain; being on foot part of each day affords close contact with the local people. "We rely on our local guides to interpret the cultural landscape as we go through," Harvey says. "We might pass a wedding party, though someone unfamiliar with Vietnam would probably not recognize this. Our guide will know, and odds are good that you will soon find yourself attending the wedding, toasting the bride and groom!"

Your walking exploration of Vietnam begins in Dalat, which lies at nearly 5,000 feet. Once a popular vacation retreat for French colonials, Dalat features rugged hills that contrast with the gentle seascape many visitors equate with the country. Your quarters will be at the Sofitel Dalat Palace. On this leg of the trip you'll visit a private home, where the residents, Mr. and Mrs. Quy, prepare a lunch from local produce.

From Dalat, you descend through pine forests and banana plantations to the coastal resort town of Nha Trang and the recently opened Evason Hideaway, a Six Senses property. The hotel stands on a rocky peninsula in Nha Trang Bay and can only be reached by speedboat. The villas—some set on the beach, some on ledges over the water, some on the hillside—include a living room, full bath, outdoor deck, and private plunge pool. After a quick boat ride to the mainland, your walk the next morning will pass through several fishing villages dotted with traditional basket boats, weaved from reeds.

Next you'll fly north to visit Hoi An, once a thriving port city that's been preserved by government authorities to capture its heyday as a trading center, a place where Chinese, French, Dutch, and Japanese cultures intermingled from the fifteenth to nineteenth centuries. Here you'll attend a morning cooking class with vivacious Ms. Vy, one of Hoi An's leading restaurateurs, at her Morning Glory Cooking School. First she will lead your group through the local markets to collect ingredients; back at the restaurant, she'll help you prepare them. Depending on Ms. Vy's whim, you may prepare crispy tuna with tamarind sauce or a street-food favorite like fresh rice paper with grilled pork.

Driving north, you will visit Hue, once the dynastic capital of Vietnam. Though many of its historic structures were damaged or destroyed in what locals call "the American War," some—like the royal tomb of Minh Mang, a complex of palaces, temples, and pavilions spread among brilliant gardens of frangipani and lotus blossoms—remain intact. One of the trip's gastronomic highlights comes in Hue. "There's a couple here that's part of old Vietnamese nobility," Harvey says. "During the war, they were both sent to reeducation camp and lost everything. About ten years ago, the husband began building a house in the architectural style of Vietnamese royalty, all by hand. In the meantime, his wife took an interest in cooking royal dishes, which have great cultural significance. This couple hosts a dinner for us in their restored home. Dishes might include minced shrimp wrapped around a piece of sugarcane, rice-flour 'cake' stuffed with shrimp and wrapped in banana leaf, fig salad, beef hot tile [strips of beef grilled over hot tiles at the table], sautéed water spinach with garlic, and sweet corn soup for dessert." After a walk on ancient footpaths connecting small villages outside of Hue, it's a flight to Hanoi.

One of the best ways to see the pull of old and new in the cities is to rise early. If you get up at four-thirty and head out to the fish market in Hanoi, you'll get a taste of the old Vietnam. The stall keepers are wearing conical hats. Along the way, people are jogging or playing badminton or otherwise exercising. "As the sun rises, there's a complete metamorphosis," Harvey explains. "In the space of two hours, the authentic markets give way to stalls with fake Prada."

On the last night of your stay in Hanoi, there's another memorable dinner. "We rent out the National Museum of Vietnamese History," Harvey explains, "and set up tables outside of this French colonial structure. One of Victnam's best bands—the band that plays for foreign dignitaries—performs for the group. They're playing traditional instruments and feature a fellow who must be the Jimi Hendrix of the *dan bau,* a one-stringed guitar of sorts. The band plays as we dine, and there are other entertainments—perhaps a puppeteer, or dancers in beautiful silk outfits."

Walking-tour guests get an intimate look at day-to-day life in Vietnam; here, women sell fish at an outdoor market in Hoi An.

IN THE SKY

Humankind has long aspired to flight—from Icarus's poetic flight of fancy to the Wright Brothers' very real adventures at Kitty Hawk. Today, intrepid would-be flyers are aided by the latest available technologies, as fighter-jet flights and even International Space Station travel are now open to a select few civilians. Both of these adrenaline-filled exploits are featured here. We follow Dr. Charles Simonyi from the steppes of Kazakhstan to the spacecraft Soyuz TMA to the International Space Station (orbiting the globe every ninety minutes) as he became the fifth civilian to experience orbital space travel. We also go *Top Gun* as Geoffrey Kent fulfills a lifelong dream to fly a jet fighter—and not just any jet fighter but an English Electric Lightning—at Thunder City in Cape Town.

Opportunities for civilian space travel are becoming increasingly available, and as prices become less astronomical, odds are good that many space enthusiasts will have a chance to enjoy orbital flight. Civilian expeditions to the moon or Mars may not be far away!

In Cape Town, would-be jet fighters can fly in one of the RAF's most famous planes—the English Electric Lightning.

49

Visiting the International Space Station

WHY: Who hasn't dreamed of visiting outer space? Thanks to special arrangements with Russia's space program, you can join professional astronauts/cosmonauts on an expedition to the International Space Station.

IN 2001, AMERICAN MULTIMILLIONAIRE DENNIS TITO BECAME THE first civilian to travel in orbital flight, thanks to the Russian Federal Space Agency and a U.S. company called Space Adventures, which has a partnership to purchase a seat on the Soyuz spacecraft and a ten-day spot on the International Space Station (ISS) every six months. The rocket, departing from Kazakhstan, brings one guest (flying with two professional cosmonauts/astronauts) to the ISS where they'll view Earth from space, live in weightlessness, and provide basic assistance to the professionals on research tasks.

Dr. Charles Simonyi (who, as head of Microsoft's application software group, oversaw the creation of the company's Office applications) was the fifth civilian to experience orbital space travel and spend ten days at the International Space Station. Blasting off into space takes a considerable commitment of time and resources. First, one must be in excellent physical condition to withstand the rigors of weightlessness. Simonyi was in good shape when he initially signed on but underwent additional conditioning—cardio, weight training, and swimming—to make sure he'd be ready to pass a prequalification exam administered by the Russian Federal Space Agency.

The next preparatory stage for civilian astronauts is a trip to the Yuri Gagarin Cosmonaut Training Center in Star City, Russia. Training exercises include mock launch and reentry simulations, and drills covering a number of mission-specific tasks you'll need to master to gain a level of self-sufficiency. These might include conducting radiation measurements and taking biological cultures from surfaces in the station. Much of the training, however, involves mastering the normal tasks of living in a state of weightlessness. The Russian estimate for minimal training for civilian space visitors is one thousand hours. "My astronaut indoctrination was one of the most

The view of Earth and the International Space Station.

enjoyable aspects of the overall experience," Simonyi says. "In the course of my training, which included interviews with dozens of astronauts and cosmonauts, I got so much advice that nothing really surprised me once I was airborne."

As the countdown ensued and the Soyuz TMA prepared for liftoff, Simonyi was taken by the new-car smell of the spacecraft ("More pleasing than the simulators!") and the sounds that indicated flight was imminent. "A noise came up from below like a bunch of rusty machine tools starting up," he describes, "and I felt a force like a helicopter taking off with maximum power. Then I felt the pressure of our acceleration, nothing out of this world—like a Corvette in first gear. Soon I could hear the stem of the supersonic shock wave moving down on the shroud of the rocket, like a bunch of crazed drummers marching by, as we passed through the sound barrier."

As the spacecraft reaches orbit some 200 miles above earth, it achieves a speed of over 17,000 miles per hour. At this velocity, the Soyuz TMA circumnavigates the earth every 90 minutes. "The earth seemed to be going by fast in front of my window," Simonyi says. "It was very blue, majestic, with a lot of white clouds. At the edge I could see the layers of the atmosphere in different shades of azure, blue, and violet." One of the otherworldly thrills of space travel is weightlessness. "In the beginning, weightlessness felt as if I were surrounded by pillows from every direction, even between my arms and body. Of course, when I moved my arm, it could move, so the illusion disappeared—until I stopped moving, when it reappeared again."

After a seamless docking, Simonyi was given a tour of his home for the next ten days by the space station's three current residents—including advice on which windows offer the best views. The station is basically a long tube, like an airliner or a submarine. Different sections are separated by bulkheads with airtight seals and reflect the different eras and styles of the ISS's construction. Velcro is ubiquitous throughout, as it holds objects in place in the gravity-free environment. There's also a good deal of laboratory equipment, which is used to measure the effects of space conditions on the human body.

On April 21, 2007, fourteen days after launching into space, Simonyi donned his space suit again for the return to Earth. The space capsule detached from the ISS and began its descent. Flames flashed outside the capsule as it sped into Earth's atmosphere. A few minutes later came the tremendous jerk of the main parachutes opening. Moments after that was a single substantial crash, which signified a successful landing in the Kazakhstan steppes.

50

TOP GUN CAPE TOWN

WHY: For adrenaline junkies, what could be more thrilling than flying a fighter jet?

THERE ARE NO EXACT FIGURES THAT SPEAK TO the increase in the number of U.S. Air Force and Navy recruits after the 1986 release of the Hollywood blockbuster *Top Gun*, though the military acknowledges that there was a significant bump and even staffed recruitment booths in select theaters where the picture was showing. The Tom Cruise character's oft-quoted line—"I feel the need—the need for speed"—evokes an enthusiasm felt by many; enough so that would-be flyers the world over are willing to part with the dollar equivalent of a new economy car for an hour in the cockpit.

"I have been addicted to speed for as long as I can remember," says Geoffrey Kent, CEO of Abercrombie & Kent. "When I was eleven or twelve, I knew what I wanted to be when I grew up—a jet fighter pilot! That didn't quite come to pass, but I never gave up on that childhood dream. When Abercrombie & Kent decided to launch Extreme Adventures and wanted to include a jet-fighter experience, we identified an operator with a good reputation in Cape Town, South Africa. Before a trip becomes part of our portfolio, I do it—so I finally got my chance to fly a jet fighter. And not just any jet fighter, but an English Electric Lightning plane interceptor!"

The flights in Cape Town are made possible by Thunder City, which boasts the world's largest private jet squadron (fourteen at this writing). While Cruise and company flew primarily in F-14 Tomcats built by Grumman, Thunder City features three jet designs: the BAe Buccaneer, a distinctive strike-attack aircraft, favored for terrain-hugging operations; the Hawker Hunter, one of the finest fighter jets ever built, and once the backbone of the Royal Air Force's fighter squadron; and the star of the lineup, the English Electric Lightning, widely considered Great Britain's most charismatic jet fighter, a supersonic plane built to intercept and neutralize cold-war interlopers. The Lightning is acclaimed for its vertical-climb capabilities; it can reach an initial climb rate of 50,000 feet per minute.

Flying a military jet is a bit more complicated than sitting down in first class on a 767 and ordering a cup of coffee. First, you need to be fitted for a flight suit and helmet. Then you receive three or four hours of instruction for whichever plane you've opted to fly in. There's a lot

Flight enthusiasts won't soon forget a barrel roll performed in an English Electric Lightning.

to learn—how to use the oxygen and the communications system; how to work the ejector seat if an emergency arises. "The thought of ejecting is a bit nerve-racking," Kent adds, "as you take on seven g's in the process!" Thunder City offers several basic itineraries, and you'll discuss preferences with your pilot—a supersonic climb, an acrobatic program, or perhaps a few passes over the cape coastline or Swartberg Mountains.

During his visit to Cape Town, Geoffrey Kent built toward the crème de la crème, first flying the Hawker Hunter, then the Buccaneer. "After these preliminary flights, I was ready for a real testosterone-charged trip, the English Electric Lightning," Kent says. "I donned my flight suit, and the Lightning was out there on the tarmac, with the canopy to the cockpit open. The pilot and I climbed in on our respective ladders, and I took the copilot's position, on the right. After we'd strapped ourselves in, the pilot engaged the first engine, then the second, with an incredible roar. We soon taxied out to the runway. As we're idling on the runway, the canopy of the cockpit slapped down, and I was told to put on my oxygen mask. The anticipation was unbelievable.

"With another roar of the engine, we accelerated down the runway, and in seconds we were off. Shortly after taking flight, the plane went vertical; in the next minute, we gained forty thousand feet (nearly eight miles), taking on five g's in the process. We achieved a top speed of Mach 2.2—fifteen hundred miles per hour! When we reached the height of our flight path—sixty thousand feet—the pilot began leading the plane through corkscrews, and then barrel rolls. From this altitude, I could see the curvature of the earth."

After an hour in the air—more barrel rolls and corkscrews, a few jaunts across the countryside—it's time to bring the plane back in. English Electric Lightnings aren't great on fuel economy—they burn 2.5 tons of jet fuel per hour. But you squeeze a great deal of excitement from your modest miles per gallon. "Before we landed, we came in over the ocean at an altitude of about fifty feet, at a speed of seven hundred miles per hour," Kent describes. "The sea was rippling, thundering below us. When we touched down, a parachute was deployed. When I deplaned, my legs were wobbly—a mix of the g-force and my nerves."

IF YOU GO

IN HARRIMAN'S WAKE: CIRCUMNAVIGATING ALASKA Cruise West (888-851-8133; www.cruisewest .com). Northbound trips begin in Vancouver, British Columbia; southbound trips begin in Anchorage.

ULTIMATE ANTARCTICA Wilderness Travel (800-368-2794; www.wildernesstravel.com) offers itineraries that include a nineteen-day expedition to South Georgia Island and Elephant Island. Trips begin and end in Ushuaia, which is reached via Buenos Aires, several expeditions are offered each year between December and February.

EXTREME FLY-FISHING IN THE CHILEAN FJORDS Nomads of the Sea (www.nomadsofthesea.com) offers its weeklong fishing adventures November through April. The trips begin and end in Puerto Montt, Chile.

EXPLORING THE GALÁPAGOS Wilderness Travel (800-368-2794; www.wildernesstravel.com). Trips begin and end in Quito, Ecuador, and are offered throughout the year.

THE SPICE ISLANDS BY *PHINISI* The *Silolona* can be booked for up to ten guests for blocks of five, seven, or nine days, through Private Label Worldwide (+44 1628 77 11 71; www.privatelabelww.com). From April to September, the *Silolona* sails from Bali to the Flores Sea/Komodo region; in October and November she sails out of Ambon, West Papua; from December to March, she sails the Andaman Sea.

MELANESIA: SWIMMING WITH MANTAS, DANCING WITH FIRE Zegrahm Expeditions (800-628-8747; www.zeco.com). Each year Zegrahm offers a different twist on its itineraries aboard the *Clipper Odyssey* in Melanesia and Micronesia, though remote islands, unique cultural experiences, and superb underwater encounters are always part of the program.

MEXICO: SWIMMING WITH GREAT WHITE SHARKS Shark Diver (888.405.3268; www.sharkdiver.com). Voyages depart from San Diego and Ensenada, Mexico.

DIVING TO THE *TITANIC* OFF NEWFOUNDLAND Deep Ocean Expeditions (www.deepoceanexpeditions .com). The trip begins and ends in Saint John's, Newfoundland; excursions are scheduled according to availability of the *Keldysh* and its submersibles (generally in the summer).

AMONG THE *MOAI* ON EASTER ISLAND Visits to Posada de Mike Rapu are available from Explora (866-750-6699; www.explora.com). The weather on Easter Island is clement throughout the year, though the warmest months are January and February.

PADDLING POLYNESIA Tahiti Expeditions (www .tahitiexpeditions.com). Moorea has regular plane and ferry service from Tahiti, where international flights land.

SURF'S UP AT SUMBA—NIHIWATU, INDONESIA Nihiwatu (+62 361 757 149; www.nihiwatu.com) accepts just twenty-five visitors at a time, only nine of whom can surf. The island of Sumba is reached via Bali; you'll need to overnight near the airport in Denpasar to catch the morning flight to Sumba the next day. You may contact Terry Simms about availability at simbasurf@yahoo.com.

ISLAND-HOPPING IN THE SEYCHELLES To coordinate the logistical challenges of island-hopping around the Seychelles, you'll be best served by engaging a tour operator like Cox & Kings (800-999-1758; www .coxandkingsusa.com). Air Seychelles (800-677-4277; www.airseychelles.net) serves Mahé.

ELEPHANT SAFARI IN BOTSWANA Abu Camp offers four-day/three-night stays. Book through Abu Camp (www.abucamp.com) or Wilderness Safaris (www .wilderness-safaris.com). To reach Abu Camp, you'll need to travel to the town of Maun on Air Botswana (800-518-7781; www.airbotswana.co.bw), which offers service from Johannesburg. From Maun, a charter flight will spirit you to Abu Camp.

RAFTING THE MOSQUITO COAST, HONDURAS
Two-week hike/float trips in the Río Plátano Biosphere Reserve in northeast Honduras are offered twice a year (July and August) by Mesoamerican Ecotourism Alliance (303-440-3362; www.travelwithmea.org). Trips depart from and end in the capital city of Tegucigalpa.

WILD BORNEO Asia Transpacific Journeys (800-642-2742; www.asiatranspacific.com) and the World Wildlife Fund (888-993-8687; www.wwf.org). The trip begins and concludes in Kota Kinabalu, Malaysia, which is served from Los Angeles by Malaysia Airlines (www.malaysiaairlines.com).

INTO THE HEART OF MYANMAR Orient-Express Hotels, Trains & Cruises (800-524-2420; www.orient-express.com). The cruise to Bhamo (described here) is offered in July, August, and September. Cruises on the lower river are available throughout the year, except in May and June. The trip begins and ends in Yangon.

ON THE TRAIL OF THE TIGER IN NEPAL
Absolute Travel (800-736-8187; www.absolutetravel.com). Conditions are best from October to March, when weather is cooler; in November and December visibility is excellent, and you can often see the snowcapped Himalayas. Most visitors reach Chitwan via a short flight from Kathmandu to Meghauli.

BIRDING IN PAPUA NEW GUINEA Ambua Lodge (+675-542-1438; www.pngtours.com) is *the* venue for visitors to Tari Valley and has naturalists on staff. Serious birders may wish to travel with a birding tour company, such as Wings (888-293-6443; www.wingsbirds.com). Air Niugini offers service to Mount Hagen, Papua New Guinea; from here, Ambua Lodge will help arrange a charter flight to Tari Valley.

ROUGHING IT ON THE AMAZON IN PERU
GreenTracks (800-966-6539; www.greentracks.com) can work with you to create an itinerary that matches your Amazon dreams. Trips are offered year-round and begin and end in Iquitos, Peru, which is served from Lima by LAN Peru.

THE GREAT-APE SAFARI IN RWANDA AND TANZANIA The Great-Ape Safari was created by Cox & Kings (800-999-1758; www.coxandkingsusa.com) and can be done alone or in conjunction with another safari adventure. The trip, which is offered year-round, begins in Kigali, Rwanda, and ends in Arusha, Tanzania.

HIKING THE CANADIAN ROCKIES The Fairmont Château Lake Louise (403-522-3511; www.fairmont.com) has 552 guest rooms overlooking the lake or the mountains of Banff National Park. Trails are generally clear of snow by early to mid-June.

A BUDDHIST PILGRIMAGE TO BHUTAN
Geographic Expeditions (888-777-8183; www.geoex .com). This trip begins and ends in Paro, Bhutan, which is served from Delhi and Bangkok. Geographic Expeditions offers other Bhutan trips, designed for trekkers and whitewater rafters.

THE MYSTERIES OF EGYPT Admiral Travel Gallery (888-722-3401; www.admiraltravel.com). The trip begins and ends in Cairo.

IN SEARCH OF EAGLES AND DRAGONS IN MONGOLIA Nomadic Expeditions (800-998-6634; www.nomadicexpeditions.com). The Golden Eagle Festival is held in October. Nomadic Expeditions leads a variety of cultural and outdoor-adventure-oriented trips in Mongolia from midspring to midfall. Trips begin and end in the capital of Ulaanbaatar.

HELI-SKIING IN NEW ZEALAND'S SOUTHERN ALPS The ski season at Blanket Bay Lodge (+64-3-441-0115; www.blanketbay.co.nz) generally runs from June through August. The lodge is open year-round with an abundance of outdoor activities for each season. Most visitors will fly into nearby Queenstown, which is served via Auckland and Christchurch by Air New Zealand.

TREKKING OMAN KE Adventure Travel (800-497-9675; www.keadventure.com) Trips run in November, December, and March, and begin and end in the capital of Muscat, which is served by many airlines, including KLM Royal Dutch and Lufthansa.

TREKKING THE INCA TRAIL LIKE A KING
Countless tour companies lead excursions of one kind or another to Machu Picchu, but only Cox & Kings (800-999-1758; www.coxandkingsusa.com) offers the coddled itinerary described here. The four-day/three-night private journey begins and ends in Cuzco, which can be reached via Lima.

COASTING ON THE KING'S TRAIL OF SWEDEN
KE Adventure Travel (800-497-9675; www.keadventure.com). A trip for seasoned Nordic skiers is offered in February; trips for skiers of all levels are offered in March and early April. The trip begins and ends in Kiruna, which has regular service from Stockholm. If time permits, consider a stay at the Ice Hotel (+46-980-66-800; www.icehotel.com).

SCALING GRAND TETON, WYOMING The Grand
Teton Climb is offered once a year from the International Campaign for Tibet (202-785-1515; www.savetibet.org). The trip is led from Jackson Hole, Wyoming, generally in August. All climbing equipment is provided.

OF ISLANDS AND OUTBACK Swain Tours (800-22-SWAIN; www.swaintours.com). The trip begins and ends in Sydney, and includes all accommodations and transportation within Australia.

PLAYING THE COURSES OF THE BRITISH OPEN The
Courses of the British Open Rota tour can be arranged by Wide World of Golf (800-214-4653; www.wideworldofgolf.com) and is generally recommended for groups of eight players. The trip begins in London and ends in Saint Andrews, Scotland.

PROVENCE BY BIKE The Cycle Provence trip
described here is offered by Butterfield & Robinson (866-551-9090; www.butterfield.com). It begins and ends in Avignon, which can be reached via bullet train from Paris.

SAVORING SIENA BY STEED The Feast of the
Conquerors ride—and other riding-oriented tours out of Castello di Tocchi—can be booked through Equitours (800-545-0019; www.equitours.com). Guests generally fly into Florence and take the train to Siena.

EXPLORING ICELAND, THE LAND OF FIRE AND ICE
H2Outfitters (800-20-KAYAK; www.h2outfitters.com). All kayaking equipment is provided. The nine-day/eight-night trip is offered in June and September.

FLOATING THE SOUL OF IRELAND Sojourns on the
Shannon Princess II can be arranged through charter brokers like Bargelady (800-880-0071; www.bargeladycruises.com). Guests will be picked up in Dublin and transferred to and from the *Shannon Princess II*.

POLAR BEAR SAFARI IN MANITOBA The Tundra
Buggy Lodge is operated by Frontiers North Adventures (800-663-9832; www.frontiersnorth.com). Trips begin and end in Winnipeg and include your flight to Churchill, which is not served by any roads. Polar bear safaris are offered in October and November.

TO THE NORTH POLE, NORWAY Polar-Explorers
(800-732-7328; www.polarexplorers.com) offers several excursions to the North Pole of varying exertion, from a multiday ski/dog-sled expedition to a champagne flight all the way to the Pole. Trips are conducted in April, when there's abundant sunlight and the ice is still thick enough to support aircraft. The trip described here begins in Oslo, Norway, and ends in Longyearbyen, Norway.

PICKIN' AT OHIO'S FUR PEACE RANCH The cast of
musicians providing stringed-instrument instruction at Fur Peace Ranch (740-992-2575; www.furpeaceranch.com) is constantly changing but always features top-tier performers. Sessions with some instructors sell out months if not years in advance.

THE PAINTED MONASTERIES OF ROMANIA
Abercrombie & Kent (800-554-7016; www.abercrombiekent.com) generally schedules trips as an extension of other tours of central Europe. Trips to Bukovina alone begin and end in Suceava; longer excursions begin in Bucharest and end in Sofia, Bulgaria.

SIPPING IN SOUTH AFRICA XO Travel Consultants
(888-262-9682; www.xotravelconsultants.com). The trip can also be conducted with a southerly trajectory, beginning in the game parks and ending in Cape Town.

THE FAIRY CHIMNEYS OF CAPPADOCIA
Tours of Cappadocia—alone or in concert with other explorations of Turkey—can be arranged through McCabe World Travel (703-762-5055; www.mccabe world.com). Most visitors will fly into Kayseri, which has regular service from Istanbul.

TEA, TANGO, AND MALBEC: FROM BUENOS AIRES
TO MENDOZA Absolute Travel (800-736-8187; www .absolutetravel.com). The trip begins in Buenos Aires and ends in Mendoza.

ISTANBUL BY *ORIENT-EXPRESS* The *Venice*
Simplon-Orient-Express (800-524-2420; www.orient -express.com) runs once a year, in August, from Paris to Istanbul and back. The train runs regularly from Paris to Venice and on other Western Europe routes. Dress is formal; a saying goes that "one can never be overdressed on the *Orient-Express.*"

THE WORLD'S GREATEST OPERA HOUSES BY
PRIVATE JET J. Q. Porter Exquisite Travel (877-JQP-8989; www.JQPorter.com). All JQP excursions are highly customizable; the many insider exclusives have been made by possible by Porter's close connections to the opera/arts world from her days as an artist and arts consultant.

INTRO TO INDIA: RAJASTHAN For her travels around
Rajasthan, Pamela Fiori retained India travel expert Cox & Kings (800-999-1758; www.coxandkingsusa .com). The city of Delhi is the best entrée point for international travelers.

MAGIC-CARPET RIDE IN IRAN Absolute Travel
(800-736-8187; www.absolutetravel.com). Female travelers should be prepared to adhere to *hijab,* the traditional code of modest dress. While the Department of State continues to warn U.S. citizens to carefully consider the risks of travel to Iran, there are no restrictions on travel.

A NIGHT AT THE BURJ AL ARAB IN DUBAI
Contact the Burj Al Arab at +971-4-3017777 or visit www.burj-al-arab.com. Dubai is served by most major carriers.

WALKING AND EATING IN VIETNAM Butterfield &
Robinson (800-678-1147; www.butterfield.com). The trip begins in Ho Chi Minh City and concludes in Hanoi and is generally offered between late January and March.

VISITING THE INTERNATIONAL SPACE STATION
Limited seats are available on future missions to the International Space Station through Space Adventures (888-85-SPACE; www.spaceadventures.com). While Space Adventures coordinates all aspects of your trip your actual host is the Russian Space Agency. Participation requires an in-depth training commitment of roughly six months. You can learn more details about Dr. Simonyi's space travels at www.charlesinspace.com.

TOP GUN CAPE TOWN Jet-fighter flights on the BAe
Buccaneer, the Hawker Hunter, or the English Electric Lightning at Thunder City may be booked through Abercrombie & Kent Space Travel (800-554-7016; www .akspacetravel.com). Interested parties will have to take and pass an aviation medical exam. A list of providers is available at Flight Physical.com.